African Essays

Colin Valentine

Published by Colin Valentine, 2024.

While every precaution has been taken in the preparation of this book, the publisher assumes no responsibility for errors or omissions, or for damages resulting from the use of the information contained herein.

AFRICAN ESSAYS

First edition. January 28, 2024.

Copyright © 2024 Colin Valentine.

ISBN: 979-8224046263

Written by Colin Valentine.

Table of Contents

Welcome to South Africa. You are now a Transvestite 1

Bed Lamps and Land Rovers 11

A Long Story About a Short Walk in Kenya 19

Death, Taxes, and Smoking Land Rovers 55

Karma hey! She's a Bitch Sometimes 67

Lost in Translation 85

The Parable of the Jacket 95

A Bit of a Rant 105

Dedication

This is for all those met along the way during travels in Africa; the good, the bad, the ugly. Some of you have made my life poorer, some richer, some harder and some easier. But that's life, and it's seldom been boring. For that I thank you no matter who you are.

Welcome to South Africa. You are now a Transvestite

I'm back in Africa. As now appears normal I had problems getting into the country. The SA immigration department has me down as an undesirable. Allegedly I've overstayed on a past visa and I'm due them substantial fines.

I dispute this. I have never overstayed a visa and I don't owe them any money. On being undesirable, there could be some truth in that.

I was confident this time. I had a virgin new passport and when last I entered SA–driving through from Namibia–the nice woman at passport control cleared the whole thing up for me and removed my name from the undesirables list–or so she told me.

This was not the case. On my arrival this trip, no sooner had I presented my shiny new passport to the wonderfully scowling immigration officer than he called an assistant who escorted me from the near clinical cleanliness of the passport control hall to a tiny room redolent with the familiar scents of urban SA–stale cigarette smoke, urine, and fried chicken. Over the next two hours, various officials took turns attempting to extract agreement and money from me. There was nothing nasty about this other than the seedy little room and the aggressive attitudes. Every half hour or so a young man in uniform would enter and scowl at me, wave my passport and a sheaf of official-looking papers in the air and inform me I had overstayed a previous visa and could not enter the country until I'd paid fines. I'd smile and explain to him he was wrong, politely requesting he go check again. Half an hour later a different scowling official would enter and we'd go through the same process. I sometimes wonder if part of the training for immigration officials in this part of the world involves 'scowling 101'.

Finally, another official appeared, a senior official I suspect. The moment she entered with my passport in her hand I knew my troubles were over. She was a woman and she smiled a lot. No shouting, no waving passport in the air, no accusations, no inflated ego. She sat and questioned me. I told her of my Namibian border experience. Satisfied with the interview she disappeared. Twenty minutes later she was back clutching a neatly stapled sheaf of papers. She led me through to the now empty immigration hall, a place that is the average tourist's first impression of SA– gleaming tiled floors, stainless steel barriers, clean air, and scowling officials. There she stamped my passport and handed me the papers. These were a printout of her investigations titled 'False Hit.' She explained she was unable to remove my name from the undesirable's list. Should I suffer the same problems on another visit I was to show these papers. Such was the warmth of her smile I decided to push my luck. I mentioned I had a domestic flight to catch and due to the delay doubted I could make the connection. Would the SA immigration department compensate me if my missed flight incurred a financial penalty?

No, they wouldn't. Still smiling she suggested I run for it. So I did.

As I jogged across the gleaming tiles of the immigration hall, the slapping of my flip-flops echoing in the emptiness, she called out, "Meester Coleeen."

I stopped and turned.

She stood, beaming at me, her face lit up as though I'd made her day. She waved and shouted, "I see you again next time!"

A sense of humour as well it appeared.

When you enter SA with an onward domestic flight booked, you can have your bag checked right through, in my case this being to East London. However, on arrival in the country, you must collect your luggage and check it through customs before checking it back in for the domestic leg of your journey.

As expected my arrival flight was no longer listed on the luggage carousel information board, my bag nowhere in sight. I went to the lost luggage desk and explained the situation. They informed me all unclaimed baggage would have been taken to the domestic desks for checking in on the owner's behalf. I didn't have time to question or dig further. Enough to say I made the flight, scraping through the aircraft's doors moments before they closed.

Luggage theft and damage is a frequent problem in SA and having not seen my bag since Heathrow I was surprised and pleased to find it waiting for me in the arrivals hall when I landed in East London.

Lindsey, my sis, was there to meet me and after a big hug, she offered to get us a coffee while I waited outside in the sunshine and enjoyed a ciggie.

As I smoked I looked down at my bag and noticed the little padlock I used to seal the zipper was missing. Alarm bells went off in my head.

I knelt and opened the bag. There was no doubt it had been gone through, everything crumpled and forced back in. Last in had been a pair of Ugg boots stuffed full of camera, battery chargers and all the dongles and leads required these days. They were nowhere in sight. When Lindsey came out with the coffees I informed her of this. I wasn't too bothered about the Ugg boots but annoyed about the chargers and leads inside them. I wasn't even sure of all I'd stuffed into them in my usual haphazard way.

Lindsey took a different view and insisted we go and make a claim which if nothing else would piss off one more scowling official. I complied and off we went to find the correct office. The official was busy on the phone so during the wait, I thought it might be a good idea to sort out exactly what was missing before taking things any further.

Opening the bag again and looking at the mess inside confirmed someone had been through the contents. My packing is never tidy but this was a mess, everything turned upside down and thrown back in. My main concern was for my hiking boots which also held various important items. They were still there. Underneath them were my Ugg boots, complete with all the things I'd stuffed into them. What the hell was going on? If someone had broken the lock then why hadn't they stolen anything? Lindsey suggested someone disturbed the thieves before they'd had the chance to take anything. Or they'd been caught and told to replace what they'd removed. I wasn't so sure, the contents were in too much of a mess.

I began to pull things out, scattering them around me, trying to remember what I should have and what might be missing. Lindsey bent forwards and delved into what little now remained in the bag. She emerged with a bra in her hand, rather a natty looking sports bra in a rather delightful shade of green. She looked at me, eyes questioning. I looked at the bra, confused. I almost felt guilty. I could tell my sis was wondering things like 'has he got a new partner? 'Is he a closet transvestite?'

I looked at her, seeing the questions in her eyes as she awaited explanation, arm extended, the bra swinging from her hand. She cocked an eyebrow.

"Anything you feel I ought to know?" she asked.

"Can't be mine" I said, "it's not my size. And besides, the colour would clash with my eyes."

We started to giggle and dug deeper into the bag. The only other item of dubious origin found was a pair of three-quarter length black Lycra jogging pants, designed for women. Not my size either.

The conclusion we arrived at was as follows.

Before my bag could be checked in for final destination as shown on its baggage ticket, it had to go through customs, with or without me there. In customs there had been several unclaimed bags opened at the same time, one of these belonging to a lady. During the repacking–if you can call it that–some items became mixed up and placed in the wrong bags. We wondered how the woman in question would react to finding a pair of my boxer shorts amid her clothing. How would her husband react?

Regardless of the many and varied sexual predilections I've entertained in the past I've never considered becoming a transvestite.

But there you go, enter Africa and it can all change, without your knowledge or complicity.

Ah, Africa. Always expect the unexpected.

* * * *

That event took place a decade ago. I still carry the 'False Hit' papers with me and every time I attempt to enter South Africa I have to produce them to avoid detention and hassle. The immigration official I'm dealing with invariably wants to make a copy for their own records, justifiable evidence for allowing me into the country even though the computer suggests I'm a heinous criminal. When this happens I request the return of the original documents as I'm sure to need them next time I enter the country. I'm assured this will happen. And every time I get handed back a sheaf of faded print papers, all mixed up, the only hint of a staple being the photocopied mark from the originals which are now in storage somewhere. Sorry.

I have asked many times why my name and alleged crimes are still on the system after a decade of coming and going in the country. I'm usually met with a shrug. I can only guess corruption is so rife nobody has the authority to remove names from overstay lists and therefore cannot accept bribes for doing so. I could be wrong.

* * * *

It's not only my alleged overstay that causes problems at borders in southern Africa. Often I have difficulties with immigration and wonder if it has something to do with my face. While others around me seem to float through without hitch I get pulled aside for some imagined contravention of law, often delayed, always admonished–after a while.

The most striking recent example happened when the concerns over COVID began to ease and a year of lock-down in South Africa was over.

I had arrived in February 2020, a month before the country went into lockdown. I was issued the usual ninety-day tourist visa. Over the next year, visitors like myself who chose to remain in the country were automatically granted visa extensions. This happened on a roughly three-month basis, the announcement usually made a month before the last extension expired. The Department of Home Affairs offices were closed for the duration of lock-down so even if you tried to renew or extend a visa it wouldn't have been possible.

Borders opened and after thirteen months in South Africa, I headed for Namibia. The last and final automatic visa extension was valid until the end of March 2021 and I was well within the time frame.

I drove north from the Eastern Cape and tested for COVID in Upington before heading towards the border post at Nakop.

The place was quiet other than for several trucks and I anticipated a rapid and trouble-free exit from the country. Dream on!

After the COVID control, I made my way to the empty departure desks and handed over my passport to the only official there. She greeted me with the mandatory scowl, leafed through my passport, then with obvious delight suggested I had a nine-month overstay penalty against me. I couldn't believe my ears.

Where had she been for the past year? Had she beamed into her desk from the planet Zog and not yet caught up with recent news? I remained calm and polite, requesting she double-check. She did. I'd overstayed my visa by nine months.

Take a deep breath. Don't become angry or show frustration. This is a simple mistake and there will be a simple solution. That's what I told myself. As usual, I was wrong.

There followed twenty minutes of arguing, me trying hard to explain how her own president had extended visa allowances during the past year of pandemic; how those who chose to remain in South Africa had been granted extensions without having to make an application, fill out any forms or stand in any queue with passport and paperwork in hand. I explained that even if they did have to do all these things then they wouldn't have managed because the Department of Home Affairs, the visa issuing authority, had been closed for the duration of lockdown and wasn't due to re-open until the end of March which happened to coincide with the end of visa extensions.

She wasn't having any of it. I had nine months overstay. She thought I was the one who'd been on the planet Zog for the past year. Could I not see that my visa expired after ninety days from entry and here I was, still in her country over a year later. What was wrong with me? Was I stupid?

I began to doubt myself, wondered if I'd got something wrong. Then I had a brain wave. Dashing out to the Land Rover I returned with my laptop and showed her a screenshot of her own government's announcement of a visa extension.

That didn't wash either. I could have made it myself. She wasn't that stupid. Did I take her for a fool? Hmmm, I'll have to think about that one.

I'm a placid person, easygoing most of the time. Now I became quite angry. The louder she shouted the louder I replied. Things became quite heated. I doubted we'd ever enjoy a quiet dinner together.

Her supervisor wandered in to see what all the fuss was about. He ignored me. It was as though I didn't exist. Not even a look or nod of acknowledgement, I was blanked completely. He stood and listened to his officer as she took him through my crimes, his head nodding in understanding, eyes watching her fingers on the computer screen as she detailed my overstay. When she'd finished he thought for a moment. From a filing cabinet, he took out a large ring binder titled 'Overstay'. Oh dear, I thought.

He laid it next to her, flipped it open, talked to her in hushed tones, taking her through the process. Then, without raising his eyes towards me he left as quietly as he'd arrived. I didn't realise it at the time but I now believe he was setting her up, allowing her to hang herself with her own rope, learn her lesson the hard way. I could be wrong.

The next ten minutes involved filling out various forms. Paperwork is still popular in much of Africa. She photocopied my passport, then settled down before her computer once more, a distinct look of smug satisfaction on her face, triumph oozing from every pore. I stood resigned, realising I'd hit a brick wall, was possibly wrong in my assumption that visas had been extended throughout the lock-down. I was confused by the whole affair.

A couple of minutes passed as she tapped away at her keyboard, eyes flicking back and forth over the screen. Then a slight frown appeared on her forehead. She tugged the earpieces from her concealed cell phone from her ears, concentrating hard now. Her frown increased, eyes darting back and forth as though to confirm what she was reading. I had to ask, curiosity, even hope, increasing with every moment.

"What exactly are you doing?"

"I am calculating your fine," she replied without looking up.

She tapped a few more keys, scrutinised her screen. Her brow furrowed and her mouth set in an angry pout. A moment later she slapped my passport back on the counter in front of me.

"You can go now," she all but spat, eyes still fixed on her screen, refusing to look up at me. My heart soared. I oh so wanted to strike a high five then do a little jig around the room. I refrained. Instead, I feigned deep concern.

"And what about my fine? How much do I have to pay?" I asked.

Her head jerked up, her face furious. If looks could kill I'd have dropped dead on the spot.

"I told you. You can go. Now GO!" she all but shouted.

"But the fine? My overstay? I don't understand," I lied.

Her eyes slit, lips thinned and pressed hard together.

"Your visa is valid until the end of March."

Deep joy.

Bed Lamps and Land Rovers

'Power-outs', a feature of life in South Africa.

A 'power-out' is a scheduled power cut. No electricity for a specified period. Details of the length and frequency of these cuts for your home area are available on the internet. Assuming of course you have the power to run your computer.

Eskom, the state power supply company, often struggles to cope with demand so they shut down certain areas at certain times of the day. In extreme cases households can be reduced to four hours of power, often when it's of least use. It might be a while before electric cars catch on in South Africa.

It's not as bad as it used to be, things are improving. The current government is doing what no previous government has attempted to do which is maintain infrastructure. Twenty-odd years of mismanagement, lack of investment and maintenance, is going to take a long time to fix. I suspect power-outs will be a feature of South African life for some time to come.

There was a time when Eskom did attempt to deal with this, in their own sweet way. As winter approached with its increased power demands, adverts would appear on television. Eskom would suggest people went out and bought blankets and candles. The power company didn't want you suffering cold and darkness. How considerate. What a wonderful solution to the problem. There were also TV adverts featuring 'power-outs' as a tourist attraction. Pretty Japanese girls stared with wide-eyed excitement at their phones, gasping 'power-out' with delighted anticipation. Such a novelty. Where else in the world could you go and not only enjoy a lack of electricity but also find information detailing when you would or wouldn't have it.

South Africans are a pretty stoic bunch, they have to be. Many found the amusing side of such inconvenience. The transition from white management to black management to power-out was explained as 'first there was white power, then there was black power, now there is no power'. The CEO of Eskom became 'the Prince of Darkness.'

But as mentioned earlier, things are getting better. Eskom management is now trying hard to correct twenty years of decay and even begin to upgrade.

It's not always Eskom who's at fault for the lack of power, at least not where my sister farms. The locals, on occasion, pop out and cut down a pole or two, bringing the lines down. Sometimes they steal these poles. Sometimes the power lines themselves go missing, these used for making illegal connections and providing power to private dwellings. Assuming there is electricity of course. Sometimes nothing goes missing which does make you question the intent behind the act.

Though you can adapt to power outs they still play on your mind, especially if you are familiar with the reliable and consistent power supply of more fortunate countries. I'll confess there have been times I would wake in the middle of the night, the room in utter darkness, and slide my hand from the warmth of the covers to click on the bedside light, to see if the electricity was working. It's amazing the little thrill of surprise and pleasure you get when the light comes on.

I'd laugh at myself when I did this, an action that reminds me of a mate over here who I teased for being such a similar type of dipstick.

This mate wanted a new 4x4–or new to him at least. High on his list of replacement vehicles was a Land Rover Defender, very much the iconic safari vehicle, but one with a reputation in this part of the world.

After months of consideration, advice seeking, poring through magazine articles and spending hours on the internet reading the good, the bad, and the ugly about his desired vehicle, he bit the bullet and bought one. It was one of those 'must have' buys, a little item of desire, something he could envision himself driving through the bush and in the desert. All the sound and sensible advice he'd received, all the articles read, all his instincts screamed at him to buy something with a better reputation for reliability. Something boring and mundane like a Toyota or Nissan. He even asked my advice which if nothing else showed desperation. I suggested he stick with Toyota and did this for two main reasons.

The first was he has a zilch understanding of things mechanical and would struggle to change a light bulb. If you ask him what happens beneath the bonnet of a car, or within the transmission, he'll look a touch vacant, think for a moment, then reply "witchcraft?".

More importantly, the seeds of doubt had already taken root in his mind. I felt that if he did buy a Land Rover then he'd never stop worrying about what may or may not happen. He would become a mechanical hypochondriac. Every rattle and squeak, every suspect hot smell, every odd clunk would set off alarm bells in his head and have him thinking the worst. His sojourns into the bush would become a worry rather than a pleasure, nightmares of concern rather than relaxing camping trips. Depending on the age and condition of the Land Rover he bought his imagination could well find plenty to fuel it.

In the end, like with most of us, his heart ruled his head. He bought a very good condition late model Defender. I felt that warm snake of envy uncoiling in my belly when first I saw it. The car he bought, though expensive, was a honey. Immaculate in fact. Even the doors closed with a reassuring thunk ... on a Defender! How do they manage that?

He invited me along on his first camping trip. Though I had no real desire to spend days listening to endless stories about how well his new vehicle was running and didn't it make mine look like a total shed (not a hard thing to do) I opted to go along. I was aware I was there as backup, to inspire confidence, this only convincing me my advice to him had been correct from the outset. But if it gave him peace of mind, allowed confidence in the new love of his life to grow, and if I could offer a little advice, impart a little knowledge, then I was happy to do it.

We went to the Karoo NP, a stunning place of soaring dolerite plateaus cloaked with red sandstone and grey shale cut deep by riverine gorges. It's a place that makes you appreciate how old the world is, how little time we have been here, and how inconsequential in the great picture of things we are. This high-altitude semi-desert with sparse and scrubby vegetation holds a surprising amount of game. I love the place, but it does have its downsides, winter being one of them. Needless to say, it was in winter we went. Like much of South Africa the winter days in the Karoo can be warm and sunny, but the nights bitter.

The campsite wasn't busy, most other guests having the wherewithal—and sense—to take a cottage with a cosy interior, wood stove and thick drape curtains. We found a secluded pitch set among a grove of trees and set up camp. For my friends, this involved a lot of all-in wrestling with voluminous amounts of green canvas, a lot of raised voices, and things called guy ropes and pegs. I unrolled my bedroll in the back of my Land Rover then snuck off to have a ciggie in peace.

That evening we braaied pork belly, potatoes and tomatoes over a bed of glowing coals. Each of us moved closer and closer to the heat as the nighttime temperature dropped and stars shone brightly in the frigid air.

Finally, it was time for bed. I snuggled deep into my down cocoon and listened to the sound of hunting jackals yipping and crying in the distance. What bliss.

Sometime during the night, in pitch darkness and hard frost, I woke to the sound of a diesel engine running. No sooner had I raised my head than the engine shut down. A moment's silence then the 'beep, beep' and flashing indicator lights as a car alarm system activated. I didn't think much of it. The crime rate is bad in South Africa. Most people won't leave their vehicles for more than five seconds without locking and double-locking them. In campsites, especially in the evenings when people are cooking, the sound of car alarms switching on and off is almost constant as necessary items are taken from or returned to vehicles. It's one of those human habits I tend to notice, especially having spent so much time in rural Scotland, Australia, and New Zealand where many leave their keys in the ignition and windows wide open. In South Africa, most people won't move more than two metres from their car without locking it. It's infuriating, especially in a campsite, often miles from anywhere and usually surrounded by an electric fence to keep wild animals out. Who in the hell is going to risk sneaking in and stealing a car? Anyhow, it's ingrained in the psyche. Justifiable I suppose.

My take on it? I'll confess I'm slap-happy. I have neither an alarm nor an immobiliser. The sound of my diesel engine starting would be enough to alarm anyone. In dodgy areas I can immobilise the vehicle by pulling a rather tatty bit of wire from the back of the ignition switch, this preventing the fuel pump from working. Apart from this, who the hell is going to steal my Land Rover? The police (assuming you could find one interested enough to bother) could outrun it with a donkey cart. I also have so little of value inside it I tend not to worry too much. And locking the doors? Hmm, I have on occasion done that, especially in towns. This sway towards caution often results in me having to break into my car, the locks refusing to open again.

Enough to say I thought little more of this late-night disturbance, rolled over and went back to sleep.

We were up before dawn, standing around the still-glowing coals of last night's fire, drinking coffee and dunking rusks in companionable silence. The electronic gates of the enclosed camp area would open at 6 A.M. and we wanted to be ready.

My invitation on this trip was on the pretence of me being the one who was knowledgeable about wildlife. A guide of sorts, free of charge. I'd expected we'd all go in the new vehicle, me reclining slothfully in the back, spouting forth about geography, geology, fauna and flora, and generally dazzling my friends with my profound knowledge and understanding. A kind of backseat David Attenborough only a bit younger and less likely to induce sleep through dulcet tones.

This wasn't to be. As we sipped from steaming mugs my mate suggested we undertake one of the several 4x4 'eco-trails' in the park. 4x4 Eco-trail … isn't that an oxymoron? He wanted me to take the lead in my own Land Rover.

I've never been into this off-roading business though I've had to do a fair bit of it. In much of Africa, roads are that in name alone. But I've never gone out of my way to do this kind of thing and like water have always chosen the easiest route. My friend wanted to test his new wheels, and probably himself into the bargain. I wasn't going to embarrass him by suggesting we all went in one vehicle. I suspect he wanted my own along for comparison, and for support should things go a bit pear-shaped.

Off-roading is a big thing in Africa. Providing you have a bottomless wallet you can deck out your vehicle with all sorts of things most owners haven't a clue how to operate, and few risk situations where they might have to. Massive chunky tyres on obscene looking allow wheels; a snorkel so you can bellow and churn screen-deep across raging torrents; great big macho bull bars with at-the-ready tow rope draped over it; high lift suspension which if nothing else makes your vehicle look big, butch and purposeful; locking differentials front, rear and centre; bumper-mounted winches; all kinds of brightly coloured red and yellow things you strap to front wings and on your 'off-road' roof rack which requires a ladder to access. All these very flash-coloured and expensive accoutrements should enable you to 'challenge nature head-on and win' ... and that kind of rubbish. I do wonder about it all, sometimes considering it a touch fetishistic. Unlike many, I don't for a moment believe these things make your dick any bigger, though I have noticed enlarged chests and heads.

Anyhow, off we set in convoy, me in the lead and more interested in the wildlife than the road ahead. We spent the day grinding up steep inclines, negotiating erosion gullies, crawling over boulder fields, and roaring through the soft sand in dry river beds. Yawn.

All went well and I did see a lot of wildlife, the highlights of my day. Another highlight was how delighted my mate was with his new love, his growing confidence and enthusiasm apparent every time we stopped for a break.

That night we celebrated with steaks grilled over the coals and more wine than was wise.

I woke in the middle of the night and for a moment lay motionless, every sense alert, wondering what had woken me in the way you do in the bush. Seconds later a diesel engine started and ran for several seconds before switching off. This time I realised the sound was very close. Sitting up in my sleeping bag I peered through the window to see my mate high-lit in the orange lights of his Land Rover's indicators as they flashed to confirm the vehicle was now immobilised. What the hell was he doing?

He went back to his tent and bed. I stuck my head back into my sleeping bag and once more drifted off to sleep, curious but no longer bothered by his rather strange behaviour.

The following day was a repeat of the first only this time I dictated the route with the allowance we did do a short section of '4x4 Eco-trail' to keep the peace. A highlight for me was a close sighting with a pair of male lions, a coalition of brothers I guessed. We came upon them unexpectedly, at much closer quarters than I'd have chosen, preferring to show some respect for the animals and not disturb them. But they appeared relaxed, unfazed by our presence and we moved on after several minutes to only a casual glance in our direction. That was an exceptional sighting in the rather vast Karoo NP with restricted visibility and undulating terrain. Fortunately, most animals, the big cats especially, find roads as useful as we do.

Even better was when only a few kilometres later I spotted a solitary male rhino not more than fifty metres from the road. I eased to a halt, indicating through my window towards where the rhino stood, aware and alert but not too concerned.

Our last night and a South African tradition for dinner, a 'potjie'. This is a very slow-cooked stew, done over coals in a cast iron pot, often never stirred from start to finish. Ours was game—Kudu in this case—with every vegetable imaginable thrown in. Though we finished early that day a potjie takes a long time to cook and again the wine flowed. Finally, I had to ask the question. What the hell was my mate doing getting up in the middle of the night and starting his Land Rover? Twice I'd heard him do it.

He looked a bit sheepish, his wife giggled. He confessed concern about the reliability of Land Rovers and the state of his vehicle's battery on these sub-zero nights. He'd left the warmth of his bed to go and start the car, to ensure it would start, to put his mind at ease.

I was a bit non-plussed. What was he going to do if it didn't start?

But now, having developed the habit of switching my bedside light on in the middle of the night to see if we still have electricity, how can I fault him?

A Long Story About a Short Walk in Kenya

There is a saying, 'Africa is not for sissies'. It holds a lot of truth. Almost everywhere you go in Africa there is poverty, hardship, a lack of education, high unemployment and crime rates. These should be constant reminders to those of us from more privileged backgrounds of how fortunate we are. For many of us travelling to Africa this situation can, and often does, instil a sense of guilt, and guilt can be played upon. In some places begging is rife, in some cases necessary. In other places it's a new form of employment, a challenging game, damned near a national sport. It's very easy to feel pressurised, even threatened, but then that's often the whole idea. Tourism, and its side benefits, have increased feelings of entitlement. Sometimes it's hard not to feel you're seen as little more than a wallet on legs, obligated to pay upon demand.

I try to give food when the need is obvious. Food is harder than money to convert to alcohol or drugs. I only give money in return for services; car guards, those who return shopping trolleys from car parks, those selling something I need. These people are trying, not expecting. At times I hand out to the very young or the very old. On one road trip, I gave my intended lunch of bread rolls and hard-boiled eggs to a couple of emaciated street urchins, bare footed and wearing little more than tatters and dust ingrained skins. Things got lost in translation as I tried to explain boiled eggs. An old lady happened along, grasped the problem immediately and explained it to the boys. She and I smiled with pleasure as they sat on the kerb and wolfed everything down on the spot with hunger so visual it was foreign.

The day I went to a large Shell station on the west side of Nairobi to collect a Suzuki pick-up hire car I didn't need to buy roses. The guy I met on the forecourt felt I did. He was small, persistent and irritating, like a bush fly that keeps buzzing in your face. In scuffed brown shoes, long trousers and a patched jacket both a size too small for him, he danced in front of me like a star footballer, obstructing my path, delaying me, and all but sticking the large bunch of red roses he was selling in my face. He'd recognised I wasn't going to buy out of need, sympathy, or white-man's guilt, so now he'd bother me like a fart in a spacesuit until I paid him to go away. It's harassment and it's very easy to become angry in these situations. It's never worth it. I kept trying to get past him, moving us both towards my intended goal, the hire car office at the rear of the fuel station's main building. He kept dodging in front of me, anticipating my every move like some prize boxer, light and nimble on his feet. He ignored my explanations of why I didn't want or need to buy, not listening to a word, shouting over me with his demands. As far as he was concerned I was going to buy, whether I wanted to or not. He'd seen me as a soft touch and he wasn't going to give up.

As we moved into the narrow space between the main building and the compound wall I finally outsmarted him. It was like being scrum-half at rugby again. I feigned left and as he went off balance to intercept me I moved fast right and past him, turning to face him and bringing us both to a halt. The change in his attitude was remarkable. In his eyes I now held the high ground. He no longer obstructed me. His whole demeanour changed to that of subservient and for the first time he was silent, his roses clutched to his chest. Once more I explained to him in a quiet, clear voice that I had no need nor desire to buy his roses. His face fell. He recognised he'd lost the battle. Poor bastard. Who else was he going to sell them to? How was he meant to eat that night? Imagine the financial loss to him if the roses wilted before he could sell them. They were only a few bucks, pocket change to me but something in his belly to him. Chances were he had a gaggle of kids to feed. I relented, my features softening and building renewed hope in his. I promised him I'd buy in a couple of weeks when I returned from my trip up north. Realising he'd lost the battle but not the war he backed off thanking me and allowing me to get on unimpeded with my day.

The Shell station was the first physical step in fulfilling a boyhood dream. I was about to depart on a foot safari in Kenya.

For years my imagination, fuelled by books, magazine articles and TV documentaries, led me to dream of a walking safari on the slopes of Mt. Kenya. The summit was also an ambition, but a secondary one.

I imagined stalking and viewing Bongo (what a lovely name), a now rare and very elusive antelope found in the high altitude forests. I'd hike through stands of prehistoric plants; groundsels and lobelias taller than a man, ancient relics found in few other places. I would fish for trout in alpine lakes, the stunning mountain backdrop reflected in their mirrored surface. I'd spend freezing nights before a blazing fire in some rustic mountain hut, sipping red wine and telling tall stories.

Those were my dreams. The reality was different, dictated as usual by circumstance and finance.

Instead of the slopes of Mt. Kenya, I took a long walk in the Laikipia district, accompanied and guided by two Samburu men, there to protect and look after me. They wore traditional red shukas tied like skirts around their waists, their feet in sandals made from old car tyres, their necks and forearms bedecked with bead bracelets suggesting their status. They were colourful, regal, imposing, and they both beamed from ear to ear.

Ben was the armed 'gun-boy' carrying an antiquated pump action 12 gauge shotgun. For ammunition, he had a handful of assorted cartridges of dubious origin and effect. His weapon, were it needed to protect us from dangerous animals, would be as much use as a chocolate fireguard. But this mattered not. Anything larger or smaller than himself frightened Ben. He was also cross-eyed.

Jon, the cook, was the opposite of Ben. He was bold as brass and afraid of nothing. But he walked unarmed. He was also stone deaf.

Our support crew consisted of two dromedary camels. These animals would carry all we needed for a week's walk in the bush. They would also at times prove awkward and slow, with a tendency to curl their lips and bare large yellow teeth before hissing in warning.

It was one of the most enjoyable times I've spent in Africa.

I was in Nairobi as part of a small team preparing cars as reconnaissance vehicles for the coming Safari Rally of Kenya. Our general factotum was Anna, a local girl there to assist in what, for us, was a strange city. On one of her regular visits to our workshop she mentioned she'd noticed I was not returning to the UK with the rest of the team but had a flight out a month later. She wondered what I intended to do with this time? I told her I wanted to see a bit more of Kenya before visiting my sister in South Africa for a couple of weeks, mentioning my dreams of Mt. Kenya but adding that my ambitions were often larger than my budget. Anna listened and asked for more detail. I explained it wasn't only lack of funds influencing my ideals. This was to be my first trip into the African bush. I was a complete novice, my only experience taken from books and the occasional movie, both of which can be romantically misleading. Though Mt. Kenya had its attractions I was open to anything available within my limited budget. If possible I wanted a taste of the true Africa, or to get as close to what remained of it as was possible in the short time available. Even if I had been able to afford it I had no desire to cosset myself in 5-star luxury and see Africa while sitting in air-conditioned comfort staring through a pane of glass. I wanted to immerse myself in the bush; to touch it, taste it, hear it and smell it—even get scratched to hell and back by it. Anna listened, took notes and said she could organise my flights but might struggle to organise a low budget walking safari, especially on Mt. Kenya. She'd see what she could do.

Courtesy of the company employing me I was lodged in the Norfolk Hotel, an icon of the safari business that reeked of colonial heydays. The original Tudor designed building is almost as old as the town itself. Its threadbare carpets, creaking floorboards, and often canted flooring reminded me of an aged aunt, doddering along in now frayed and outdated clothing, mumbling of past glories, smelling of mothballs and dust, while nibbling on cucumber sandwiches or downing gin and tonics.

Photos of eminent past patrons adorned the walls; from royalty on tour to millionaire industrialists who came to hunt big game–or Hollywood stars there to make movies about hunting big game. Robert Redford and Meryl Streep stayed in the Norfolk while filming 'Out of Africa'. When watching all the safari-going guests coming in for an early breakfast, I often had to do a double-take to make sure they weren't still in residence.

A highlight for me was the breakfast chef, resplendent in an immaculate white uniform and towering chef's cap. I was usually his first customer and he'd greet me with a beatific and infectious smile, enough to make any pressing concerns vanish from the mind, even if only for a while. He introduced me to chilli omelettes, something I'll be forever grateful for.

The Norfolk is a lovely old reminder of what Kenya must have once been like, a relic of a bygone age. It still competes with the faceless chrome and glass comforts of more modern establishments. For many, it's part and parcel of their Kenyan safari, as important as the wildlife, scenery and people.

A couple of nights after speaking with Anna, when I went to collect my room keys from reception, I was handed a large envelope. In my room I cracked a cold beer, sat down and read through several handwritten sheets of the proposed itinerary. Half an hour later I phoned and thanked her for her efforts, asking her to go ahead and book everything. She'd found cheap flights, tickets to be delivered before departure. For the same price as a couple of nights in the Norfolk, she'd organised a camel supported walking safari in the Laikipia district, and the hire of a Suzuki jeep to get me there and back. It was a no brainer. I was as hooked as one of my imaginary Mt. Kenya trout.

I knew nothing about the Laikipia district, hadn't even heard of it, but what I learned over the next couple of weeks only increased my enthusiasm. Located in the North-central part of Kenya, at 9,500 square kilometres it's the country's second-largest wildlife conservancy. It's managed by the people who live there, local communities and ranchers/landowners. Sitting on the equator this high altitude plateau is broken by forested valleys and deep river gorges, a tortured and geologically rumpled topography. The traditional pastoralists and ranchers run their livestock alongside free-roaming wildlife, endeavouring to maintain a happy balance with space for all. Back then this was a controversial conservation concept still in its infancy.

I've heard the Laikipia holds a greater number and variety of wildlife and is a better safari destination than even the well known Mara. I've never been to the Mara so I can't judge. The reason I've never been to the Mara is that for me there would be too many other people. Enough said.

Finally, the work was finished, the rally completed, and the rest of the small team departed leaving me free to indulge my ambitions.

After the minor interruption of the flower seller was over I stood for a moment and tried to regain my composure and the feelings of excitement and anticipation I'd been enjoying since Anna had confirmed arrangements. I watched him retreat to his post at the fuel station entrance, then turned and headed towards the car hire office.

The tall and imposing turbaned Sikh hiring out the Suzuki recognised me as being a soft touch as well. Before handing over the keys he took me through the many perils and pitfalls of driving in Kenya. This involved much head bobbing, eye-rolling, beard-stroking and hand waving. And some very colourful prose. Hiring a car had never been like this back home. But then we didn't have most heinously corrupt scoundrels manning police roadblocks, or nefarious villains lurking with most despicable intent at every fuel station. It was with considerable relief, and a touch of foreboding about the coming journey, that I finally waved him—and that most unscrupulous looking fellow the flower seller—goodbye and joined the dodgem-like madness that passes for Nairobi traffic.

I was almost disappointed by how uneventful the drive was. No most dishonourable officials charging on-the-spot fines, receipt unavailable. No nefarious criminal types lurking like predatory hyenas in fuel stations. Only one police roadblock where the polite officer in an immaculate uniform wished me a pleasant stay in his wonderful country. All a bit of an anticlimax.

The scenery would have been stunning, had I been able to appreciate it. Kenyan roads demand full attention at all times, and a sensible speed. The tarmac is now in disrepair, a sea of potholes some large enough to swallow a Suzuki, or if nothing else tear a wheel off. In places, it's as though these potholes have bred and now form small colonies so large that oncoming vehicles swerve in an attempt to avoid them. At times it's like playing chicken with oncoming traffic, everyone vying for the same piece of smooth tarmac. Head-on collisions are common.

What I did note was how lush, green and cultivated much of the lower-lying country is. The crop and vegetable patches were small, hand-tended rather than mechanised, separated by linear watercourses. Black women hoed or stooped and dug, their dresses of vibrant reds, blues, mauves and oranges standing out in contrast in the sea of Irish green. The air was hot and heavy, a mild sauna through the jeep's open window, redolent with the scent of rich, damp soil. The fertility in some areas was tangible. I got the impression that should the women relax their industriousness, even for a moment, then nature would reclaim with delightful disorder.

The route I took, as per Anna's detailed instructions, curved around the southwest of Mt. Kenya, still snowcapped and dominating. It looked out of place, as though it shouldn't have been there. The mountain is the reason for the fertility, providing washed down alluvial soils and a steady flow of water. The place is going to suffer when that snow cap is no longer.

After a while, I headed northwest, elevation increasing, the air cooling and drying. Cultivated greens dropped behind, replaced by craggy valleys and towering koppies of tumbled red rock standing in seas of dry bush. The ground became bare and stony, green lost its vibrancy, and brown and grey became common. Thorn became the norm. After the almost manicured order of the lower, more productive lands these had an untamed feel, a sense of wildness. This was the Africa I wanted to be in.

Outside the town of Rumaruti, once the capital of Laikipia, the road turned from potholed tarmac to potholed gravel. Anna's last handwritten route instruction suggested I follow this road for twenty-one kilometres. When I spotted a huge boulder on the right with a yellow painted arrow pointing left, I was to follow it. I found it and I did, turning left onto a steep two-track. I bumped and rattled my way to the top of an escarpment and the large clearing in the bush where I was to meet my cameleers and their camels. The place was deserted, hardly surprising considering I was four hours late. I took a good look around, stretched cramped muscles, then sat down on a rock and lit a ciggy. It was then I noticed I was being watched from the far side of the clearing by a white guy of about my height and build. He stood legs spread, hands-on-hips, glowering at me from beneath the frayed rim of a faded, once green bush hat. His T-shirt hung ragged and his shorts were old fashioned short shorts. At the ends of his tanned and dust-powdered legs were tennis shoes with the toes cut out. He didn't look happy. He did look feral.

"You must be Colin. You're late," were his introductory words. The story of my life I thought. I was eighteen days overdue at birth, something my mother appeared to believe was intentional and never forgave me for. I've been trying to catch up ever since. I explained and apologised as we shook hands. John was the rancher who ran camel safari's as a sideline.

It was too late in the day for me to begin walking, the cameleers and camels already sent home. Instead, I'd spend the night at his campsite and begin the walk the following morning.

With John in the passenger seat giving directions we followed a maze of dusty two tracks through the bush. It was obvious I wasn't flavour of the month but we chatted nonetheless. The moment I mentioned I'd been a cattle farmer in Scotland all seemed forgiven. John had found a new friend, someone who shared his interests and understood their complexities without the need for detailed explanation. Someone he could relate to. As Amanda, John's wife, put it later that same evening, he'd found someone he could kidnap and talk cattle farming at. It was a case of 'cattle break ice'.

I don't wish to bore you with facts about cattle farming but I would like to give one example that suggests the differences between Kenya and Europe and gives a picture of what Kenya is all about. I farmed two rented units in the foothills of the Grampian mountains. It was an average operation for the area and carried one hundred and twenty hill cows producing an annual crop of calves sold on to the fattening market. John's ranch carried over four thousand head of cattle. Recently he'd lost one thousand five hundred head during a drought. Staggering. Economy of scale.

We parked up behind an old Land Cruiser sitting next to what I realised had once been a high diamond mesh fence, now so overgrown with creepers and vines it blended in.

I followed John through a gate and down an overgrown path. His house appeared as if out of nowhere so well did it fit into the surroundings. Built of eucalyptus poles and plastered with a mix of the native soil it looked like part of the koppie it stood against, the rock forming the back wall. Some of the windows were standard glass while others were made out of the bases of wine bottles set in tight clusters into the wall.

At the small door two labradors, one black and one gold, met us. Both were ecstatic to see their master and even more excited to have someone new to sniff and provide attention. We were also met by a small, grey monkey that hurtled towards me, teeth bared and eyes ablaze with hatred, chattering with rage.

"Don't worry about Monkey," commented John over his shoulder, "he does that to everyone until he gets to know you. He's testing you out, seeing if he can make you jump."

Monkey succeeded in his efforts and appeared quite pleased with himself.

Inside, I settled on an ancient couch, the seat cushions supported from beneath by piles of old newspapers and farming magazines. Two cats appeared, leaping onto the arm of the couch, purring and rubbing their cheeks against me. The dogs leapt up and settled, one on my lap, the other leaning hard against my shoulder. I felt quite at home and very welcome.

From a large and ancient-looking kerosene fridge that wobbled when he opened the door, John took a couple of bottles of beer, popped the tops and handed me one.

"Sorry it's a bit warm," he commented, "bloody fridge hasn't worked for years."

"So why do you keep it?" I asked, the words out of my mouth before my brain was in gear.

"Where else would I keep my beer?"

There is a strange logic to this. Kenya logic as I was beginning to learn.

I'm going to digress for a moment. The following section contains descriptions of actions some people may feel are unacceptable. I did consider making no mention of these events but opted to include them on the basis they are part of the story. Disclaimer: No person or animal suffered harm during these events, or in the telling of them.

Should you find some of the following not to your tastes then it's simple. Stop reading. You're not under any obligation, try to remember that.

Every time I look back on what took place I'm reminded of the pub sport of 'dwarf throwing'. This began in Australia, which sounds right. It is the kind of pub game Australians would invent and glory in. Dwarfs or midgets, people of restricted growth, are hurled, tossed, thrown, usually onto soft mattresses. The person who hurls the dwarf furthest wins. In more imaginative events the dwarf dons a velcro suit and gets hurled at a velcro wall. I've read that some dwarfs even enjoy sitting on a skateboard and taking the place of a bowling ball.

Needless to say, well-meaning people who feel entitled to interfere have attempted to ban these activities. Shouldn't that be the choice of the individual dwarf?

But I digress. Back to the story. You've been warned.

So, John and I talked about cattle farming. John wanted to know all about how things worked in Scotland, I wanted to know about ranching in Kenya. Another beer was enjoyed and by the end of a couple of hours we were getting on like a house on fire.

"Fancy a walk?" asked John. "I always walk the dogs this time of day, when it's cooler."

I'm always up for a stroll and was keen to see some more of the kind of bush I'd be walking through over the next few days.

As we left the house, the dogs streaming past us in excited blurs, Monkey leapt onto John's shoulder and sat there baring teeth and chattering at me. It appeared Monkey came on walks as well.

Still in the garden area, within the perimeter fence, John veered off the path and began peering into and under bushes.

"There's a cheetah in here somewhere. Give me a hand to find her will you."

Of course there is I thought. Doesn't everyone have a cheetah in their garden? I stilled the 'What!' that waited in my throat and joined John in the search as though I did this kind of thing most days of the week, thinking it possible many Kenyans did. Moments later I noticed something long and straight and very un-branchlike hanging out of a tree. My eyes followed it upwards to find it attached to the rear end of quite a large spotted cat reclining Sphinx-like along a horizontal branch, looking down at me with casual disdain.

"Is this what you're looking for John?" I called.

He appeared next to me, Monkey chattering on his shoulder, both of them looking upwards to where the cheetah lay looking down on them with an air of studied detachment. John called a couple of times. I learned the cat's name was Cheetah. Stands to reason, doesn't it. Monkey and Cheetah. Should we bump into a tame elephant I'd now have a good idea what its name might be. John called louder, a human trait I've noticed with many dog owners. 'Come here immediately Rex, or next time I'll shout louder!' kind of thing. John's increase in volume had about the same effect as this behaviour has with most dogs. No response other than a wide yawn from the cat, its long pink tongue extended and curling with nonchalant disinterest as it observed those below with the aloofness only a cat can muster. Cursing, John took a step forwards, grabbed the end of the long tail and gave it a good hard tug. That did the trick and in a trice Cheetah joined us on the ground.

The dogs rushed around the cat with joyous excitement as though greeting a long lost friend. Monkey chattered and pulled at John's hair, jumping up and down on his shoulder with fiendish-like glee. It did flash through my mind that if I ever wrote about this episode no one would believe me. Little did I know there was more to come.

Ten minutes of walking along a narrow dirt track took us to a small enclosure, the walls built with local stone. They reminded me of the stone dykes used to enclose fields in my native Aberdeenshire, a place that seemed a million miles away at that moment in time.

"This is our sanatorium," said John, "where we keep sick animals so it's easy to check up on them, doze them, that kind of thing."

I climbed up the high wall and peered over. On the far side of the enclosure lay two camels. They looked relaxed and unconcerned, their backs against the wall for the best shade, large dark eyes fringed with long curved lashes, slow working jaws as they chewed the cud. For a couple of minutes we chatted about the animals and the ailments afflicting them. The dogs circled and whined with impatience, wanting to get on with the walk. Monkey inspected John's hair for lice or fleas, grooming him. We went to move on then noticed Cheetah was no longer with us. John cursed and peered over the wall as though he knew already where the cat would be. I followed suit to see Cheetah, already inside the enclosure, now ever so carefully stalking one of the unperturbed camels. For several seconds the cat stood motionless, not a twitch, long tail relaxed and hanging, neck extended and head held low, ears back, eyes locked on her prey. She looked like a statue. The camel continued to chew the cud, long eyelashes flickering, no sign of alarm whatsoever. Then it turned its head and Cheetah took one slow step closer before freezing mid-stride.

"Bloody cat," mumbled John, climbing onto the top of the wide stone wall and hurling a rock, hitting her on the haunch. The cat didn't even blink. Camel (I'm making a wild guess at the name) chewed the cud and looked bored with the whole affair, an affair I got the impression it may already be familiar with. John shouted curses and Cheetah ignored them. He picked up another rock and the cat turned her head to look at him. He raised his arm as if to throw and shouted again. Cheetah's body relaxed, she gave up on her game. She turned and ambled with casual grace towards us as though innocent of any bad intent. Leaping with one fluid movement onto the top of the wall next to where John stood, she closed her eyes with delight as he ruffled her behind her ears, her cheek rubbing against his knee. Camel's jaws stopped working for a moment as though the animal were thinking, concentrating. Her head turned and she looked at us quite pointedly. There was an impressive fart. Camel began chewing the cud once more.

As we walked along dirt tracks surrounded by grey thorn bush, the ground all but bare beneath, John told me about Cheetah. She was found–allegedly abandoned–in the bush and taken to him. He'd offered no reward to the finder as this would only encourage others to lift young animals from the bush and turn up with them. His family had raised the cub but all attempts to return her to the wild had failed. She had adopted them as her own and now they were resigned to keeping her for as long as she wanted to remain. John's biggest concern was she was now so conditioned to people she would be easy prey for any trigger happy hunter, even for locals who could sell her skin in the city. To this end, she now generally wore a red canvas harness which he hoped would alert anyone to the fact she wasn't wild.

Cheetah didn't appear to enjoy going for walks and tended to stroll with casual disinterest behind us. When she felt the distance was safe enough she'd slope off into the bush and lie down for a bit of a snooze. After this had happened for the third time, the dogs loving every moment of the search but John becoming frustrated with the delays, he opted to make our walk a bit more interesting for the cat. Easing Monkey from his shoulder and holding the little animal by the scruff of the neck he waved it slowly in front of Cheetah. The cat became alert, dropping her air of indifference, ears twitching as she watched John with expectation. With a long slow underarm throw John hurled Monkey into the air out in front of us. Monkey performed a perfect ark, screeching and chattering all the way, limbs splayed star-like. Cheetah bolted forwards, gone like an arrow from a bow. Monkey landed light as a feather, twisting in the air last minute to land facing the speeding cat, back feet first then front feet immediately after. As Cheetah was about to run into Monkey the little grey animal scooted between the cat's front paws and shot under her belly. Screeching like a banshee Monkey raced back to us and was sitting on John's shoulder before the cat had spun around. I was a bit gobsmacked, thinking about animal rights groups, cruelty to animals organisations, the look of shock and horror on the faces of many I knew should they observe this practice. Then I looked at Monkey, then at Cheetah. It dawned on me both were enjoying the game, anticipating more. It was a bit like throwing a stick to entertain a dog, except it wasn't. Or hurling a delighted dwarf.

Monkey sat on John's shoulder, chattering away as though shouting taunts and insults at the cat. Cheetah strolled back towards us, looking a little less cocky than before, her head turned upwards to look at John. John obliged her, once more taking Monkey from his shoulder. I noted the little animal didn't even attempt to grab a handful of his hair or resist in any way. The ritual was repeated, Monkey arching through the air, limbs spread wide, screaming indignation, landing effortlessly and scooting beneath the pouncing cat to rush back and perch on John's shoulder, chattering with excitement. The dogs barked and rushed around with delight, as familiar with this game as the protagonists were. I wondered who they backed, Monkey or Cheetah?

Twice more Monkey was sent soaring and twice more Cheetah failed in her attempts to catch the little animal. I don't think she had any real intention of doing so but enjoyed the game for the game's sake. Finally, Monkey had enough. He chose me for sanctuary. Springing from several metres away he landed with surprising lightness against my chest. In a flash he scrabbled up and onto my shoulder, wrapping his little arms around my head so I could feel his heartbeat against my cheek. Cheetah sauntered up and looked at me with expectation.

"Have a go," said John, "throw him if you want, he loves it."

I didn't have the heart. Besides, Monkey appeared to have accepted me and I didn't wish to give him further reason for attacking me next time I appeared at the house.

Darkness comes fast on the equator and we returned to the vehicles and garden gate as it fell. A huge figure stepped from the shadows and John spoke with him in Swahili. He was massive, a man-mountain dressed in green one-piece overalls and short rubber boots, a pump-action shotgun slung over one wide shoulder. His bullet head was shaven smooth and glistened in the failing light. Most impressive were his earlobes. These were stretched until they hung to his shoulders, each with a hole I could have put my fist through. I caught myself staring with amazement and found him staring back at me with equal fascination. But then again I did have a monkey sitting on my head investigating my short hair for parasites. I like to think it failed in the quest.

John informed me this man was to be my bodyguard and would now escort me to a shower and my accommodation for the night. When I was ready he'd take me back to the house for dinner.

I followed Man Mountain (my name for him) down a long winding path, his torch lighting our way. My accommodation was a small rondavel with mud walls, a thatched roof, and a door that hung on one hinge. I dropped my bag on the single bed, grabbed my towel and soap and followed MM to where I was to shower. The shower block was, if viewed from above, a simple 'S' in shape with one of the curves housing a shower for the ladies, the opposite side for the men. Hot water came from a 'donkey boiler'. That's not to say it boiled donkeys. A 'donkey boiler' is usually a home-built steel affair where a wood fire heats a tank of water. This one had been lit earlier, the fire now all but burnt out but the water still piping hot and with plenty of pressure. I wondered when John had arranged this because he hadn't spoken with anyone other than me since I'd arrived. MM took his duties seriously and seated himself on a rock nearby while I showered in full view of him. I suspect John had stressed that I wasn't to be allowed out of his sight. I dropped my western reservations along with my boxer shorts and showered, washing off the dust and sweat of the day. Later I asked John why the need for MM and his pump-action shotgun, thinking it was for protection against roving wildlife. He replied that was part of the reason. They also had occasional problems with 'shifta', a legacy of Somali/Kenyan conflict still not resolved.

After a chicken dinner we drank more beer and talked about farming. When I rose to go John escorted me to the door and out of the garden's thick vegetation appeared MM, complete with large flashlight and pump-action shotgun. We walked to my rondavel outside of which a small fire already blazed. This was where MM would spend his night, sitting beside it. Ten minutes later I was in my sleeping bag and sound asleep.

Sometime during the night I awoke with a pressing urge to pee. I didn't bother with a head torch but rose and lifting and scraping the one hinged hanging door open I stepped into the moonlight. There was no sign of MM at his fire so I stood on the edge of the stoep and began peeing into the bushes below. Mid flow a light flicked on, shining over my shoulder. It was MM who'd appeared without a sound from behind me and was now assisting me to take a piss, allowing me to see where my stream was falling. There's not a lot you can do in these situations so after the momentary fright of his appearance I continued as though he wasn't there.

When I slid back into my sleeping bag I noticed a kind of munching noise coming from somewhere close by. Several times I switched on my head torch, looking for the source of this continuous feast. I never saw a thing but when I mentioned it to John the following morning he told me it was white ants eating the roof thatching.

After a very early breakfast, John was keen to show me some of the ranch. He had a captive audience and he wanted to make the most of it. I was more than happy to go along with this, my itinerary loose and my interest genuine.

One of the things that impressed me most was a large, unfenced area where he kept his prize bulls. These were huge, powerful beasts with a hump of fat above their shoulders and a heavy dewlap, storage areas for times of drought. They made the Aberdeen Angus and Simmental bulls I was familiar with appear light-weights. Each free-ranging bull had its herder, a young boy wearing little more than a loincloth and beads. Some of these kids weren't ten years old and no taller than the bull's front legs. Each carried a thin wand cut from a tree. When they wanted the grazing bull to change direction or move elsewhere they would tap the animal on the nose with this wand. Simple and effective. I did wonder why in Europe we use halters and nose rings, electric cattle prods and steel races when all you need is a half-naked child with a bit of bendy stick. Different cultures. Different methods of husbandry. A more intimate relationship with your livestock.

Finally, and with touching reluctance, John released me from hospitable captivity and the walk began. Ben took the lead, shotgun over his shoulder, towing the first camel with a rope halter. From this camel's tail led a thin cord attached to the second camel's nose peg. Jon followed, encouraging the animals along with soft words. I wandered along behind him. This was how we would travel for the duration of the safari.

The days fell into place, routine replacing initial uncertainty as it does. On that first afternoon, as on every afternoon that followed, we found a suitable campsite before the heat of the day. This was usually a patch of thick bush on higher ground with open grassland surrounding it. Ben and Jon, using machetes, would hack a clearing in this bush, creating enough space for a fire, storage and sleeping areas. The camels, on command, would lie down to have their packs and saddles removed and laid out beside the fire area. Now hobbled they were free to browse until twilight. We'd gather enough deadwood to last the night. A fire would be lit and tea brewed before we selected our sleeping areas; Ben and Jon close to the fire, me a respectful distance from them. We'd lay out our bedrolls and doze the hottest part of the day away in somnolent silence.

Late in the afternoon, we'd rise. More tea would be brewed. Then Ben, armed with his trusty old 12 gauge, would take me for a stroll in the bush.

Though we often saw game during the day, sightings were more common in the cooler hours of dawn and dusk when many prey species choose to feed. Kudu, impala, Grant's and Thompson's gazelles, and the occasional bushbuck were the most commonly seen as Ben and I walked quietly along. It was the kudu that impressed and thrilled me the most. I found them beautiful to behold, considered them ambassadors of the bush with the ability to vanish into what seemed impenetrable vegetation with not a sound. Giraffes have a serene majesty all their own and made me think of graceful sailing ships whenever I saw their long necks swaying above the flat-topped acacias as they moved away. And elephants. Who can not feel moved by their first sighting of elephants while on foot? One evening we crested a low ridge to find a single bull elephant standing close by a water hole not far below. We watched him for long minutes, standing in silence, our presence undetected. He was motionless, his head supported by his straight trunk as though it had become too heavy for him, the weight of his thick, curving tusks now more a nuisance than a benefit. He was lost in reverie, and I wondered what he thought about. It was obvious even to me he was an old fellow and I liked to imagine he was standing there remembering his past life, all the adventures and travels he'd enjoyed, all the lovely ladies he'd mated with, all the healthy young calves he'd sired and disciplined and taught, passing on not just his genes but his accrued knowledge and his codes of elephant etiquette. After many minutes he came out of his trance, lifting his head and shaking it so his ears flapped against his neck, raising dust and making a sound like clapping hands. With slow grace, he turned and shambled off into the trees, an old man in grey, baggy, wrinkled pants.

I enjoyed the morning walks most of all. With no distractions and little else to do, we bedded soon after darkness and rose before dawn. Before the sun had begun to lighten the sky Jon would be up tending to the fire and putting water on. Draped with blankets or sleeping bags all three of us would huddle close to the now blazing warmth, dunking biscuits in hot sweet tea and eating fruit.

As the sun began to light the sky I'd use a little of our precious water to wash away my sleep before Ben and I set off on our morning stroll while Jon packed up the camp.

The air was still cool, fresh and clear before the heat of the day turned it into dust tainted shimmers. The world felt new. We had no set destination, no set purpose other than to walk and see some country, our only time frame was the return date. It was relaxed, and oh so enjoyable if only because of that lack of needing to do, see, be somewhere. I consider myself very lucky in that much of what I've seen, be it wildlife or country, has been part of an 'everyday' rather than a specifically pursued novelty.

Ben could read the ground and the bush in the way you or I read a newspaper. Shotgun slung over his shoulder he'd use his stick to point out fresh tracks, dung, urine stains, even feeding signs on grass or bush or tree. As he pointed he'd say the English name for the animal responsible; kudu, impala, elephant, zebra, giraffe, jackal and so on, providing more information than my poor brain could cope with. I'd anticipated seeing and experiencing with a little bit of learning but much of what Ben did his best to point out and explain was lost on me. When we spotted game before the animals were aware of us we'd become little boys, testing our skills and seeing how close we could get before the animal's heads jerked up and ears began to rotate back and forth as they tried to pick up the direction the noise came from.

Regardless of being a greenhorn, I could still discern the theatre Ben included in our walks, often making more of a meal out of a straightforward stalk than was necessary. I concluded this was to impress and instil the belief that without his guidance–and superior bushcraft–success would have been negligible. I also suspected the prospect of a large tip at the end of our safari may have been another dangling carrot encouraging such performances, but played along with his theatrics and rather enjoyed them.

It was the same at night when having eaten, communicated as best we could with sign language, pidgin English, facial expressions, grunts, groans and mimes, all this very much like playing after dinner charades, we'd retire to our respective sleeping sites. Ben and Jon, with only blankets for warmth, would settle by the fire, the camels close by. I, with my light down sleeping bag, would choose a spot further from the heat. I would lie awake, smoking, listening to the night noises of the bush which never seems to sleep, staring with wonder at a night sky unfamiliar to northern European eyes. A vast blanket of deep black pinpricked by a hundred thousand stars, the great belly bulge of the milky way curving across it all like pale wisps of woodsmoke.

Often, as I lay there wondering in the way you do, about life on distant planets, the sheer vastness of it all, how inconsequential we are, Ben would put on a performance which I'm sure was for my benefit. With a start he'd sit bolt upright, a figure of alert concern. He'd shine his flashlight (another item he was very proud of) into the darkness, sweeping the beam back and forth as though searching for potential threat, imagined or otherwise. He'd raise his shotgun, shoulder it while still sitting, sweep the barrels back and forth, covering the approach to our camp as though expecting predators to appear. In ways I found this disconcerting. Not because I viewed it as a charade designed to impress and put me at ease, but because Ben's gun never seemed to point in the same direction as his eyes.

Satisfied we were not about to be devoured in our sleep he'd turn towards me, aware he'd had an audience. He'd smile and nod as though to reassure me all was well and I was safe, Ben was on the job and I could sleep soundly.

All this was theatre, done for effect and that anticipated tip. Never once did I hear or sense a presence outside the firelight, or see eyes reflected in the flashlight's beam. I did see two camels hobbled for the night, lying close by the edge of the firelight, heads raised on long necks like the periscopes of submarines, chewing the cud, huge soulful eyes blinking beneath long feminine lashes. I felt confident that had there been a threat out there they would have known.

For all his theatrics Ben was a skilled and knowledgeable guide who did his best to share his knowledge with me. The variety of animals and the signs identifying them were so numerous I realised I could never absorb it all in the short period of time available so best to enjoy it for what it was, an enlightening walk in some wild country. Or at least I thought it was wild until I began to run low on cigarettes.

We'd been out for several days, walking for six hours each day and covering considerable distance. In all that time we'd only seen one other person, one of John's cattle guards who appeared on an ancient bicycle one night, rattling out of the darkness and into the light of our campfire. From his handlebars swung a bright yellow, five-litre plastic container that had once held Shell 20W40 Motor Oil. It now contained curdled milk, a gift for Ben and Jon. Introductions over, our guest joined us by the fire. The oil container opened with an ominous hiss of escaping gasses, and then passed from smiling face to smiling face, until the dreaded inevitable happened and it was offered to me. I'll confess I wasn't enthusiastic. I was curious, and I didn't want to offend—or lose face. All eyes watching me, faces smiling with amused expectation (no pressure there), I raised the container to my lips with both hands. The smell alone was disconcerting. I took a good slug, paused, and then took another before handing the container back. I feigned relish as I wiped the froth from my lips with the back of my hand. The looks of amazement almost made the ordeal worthwhile. I decided soured milk was an acquired taste. The container circulated and the guys chatted. Once more it was offered to me. I declined but thanked them and they smiled in understanding. I hadn't fooled anyone but at least I'd given it a try. I did consider cracking a joke, stating it wasn't my grade, I preferred 10W50. It would have been lost in translation.

Considering the visiting cattle guard was the only person we'd seen so far, no sign of habitation, no smell of woodsmoke, only the occasional jeep two-track through the bush, I did believe we were remote, in the middle of nowhere.

After one of our early morning walks, as we sat enjoying coffee before setting off for the day, Ben noted I was running low on cigarettes and had been rationing myself. He didn't miss much. If I wanted to buy more there was a village only a few kilometres away. He could be there and back in a couple of hours while I remained in camp and relaxed.

A village I thought! That came as a bit of a surprise. And then it dawned on me. Ben and Jon, knowing the area well, had avoided all human presence. They knew I didn't want it, only bush and wildlife of which we'd seen plenty. John's ranch ran on people and provided them with work. Each and every family was responsible for a number of both small and large stock. Of course there had to be people about, many people, and people need stuff which means a store of some sort. Africa had always been this way and it was my preconceived ideas and wishful thinking that had prompted me to consider it empty other than for wild animals. Back in the day the locals had lived alongside wildlife, not always in harmony but co-existing nonetheless. Things hadn't changed. This was Africa, very much as it always had been, and scattered settlements were very much part of it all.

I opted to walk with Ben rather than remain in camp. For almost an hour we followed the course of a river, making frequent stops to look and listen hard for signs of danger ahead. On one of these halts, as we stood in silence, the loud cracking of breaking branches came from somewhere off to our left. Ben stilled my question by holding his hand up, demanding silence, his face a mask of concern. The cracking came again and this time, ready for it, we both raised our hands and pointed in the same direction.

"Elephants," hissed Ben and dropped down to squat behind the cover of a bush. I followed suit and together we peered through the vegetation towards where the sounds were coming from. It was a small herd of cows with calves, ambling past at about eighty metres distance.

I didn't know a lot but I did know mothers with children tend to be very protective, often aggressive. A common perception is that it's the male of the species one has to be wary about; the raging bull, the heavy maned lion ... that kind of thing. In my experience it's not the males you have to worry about, it's the females with offspring. During my farming years I was butted by sheep, treed by a sow with piglets, and often had to sprint for the safety of my pick-up truck when ear tagging recently born calves. The mothers were out to get me. Never once did I have to run from a ram, bolt from a boar, or bugger-off from a bull. Male aggression usually only appears when a challenge for harem or territory arises, and then usually from the same species. Mothers with children consider anything as a potential threat and this is common throughout nature. Crocodiles, generally viewed as 'cold blooded', emotionless, soulless reptiles, hang about their nesting area, protecting it from predators until the hatchlings emerge.

The mother will often then transport these hatchlings to water, in her mouth. Female octopuses remain close by their egg clutches, not eating or moving, protecting their unhatched offspring and dying in the process. Rule No 1 in the bush, or anywhere else for that matter, is never get between a mother and her offspring. Mums are usually fearless protectors.

All this was going through my head as we knelt behind the bush and watched the elephants browsing and breaking their way by. I assessed the situation as best my limited experience and knowledge allowed. The elephants were distant and their casual feeding behaviour suggested they were unaware of us. The light but steady breeze was blowing from them to us. I could smell them. If smells had colour an elephant's would be mouldy green, like rotting vegetation. They were moving in the opposite direction from ours and though browsing without haste would be gone in a few minutes. We were in no rush, we could wait until they'd passed before moving on. The narrow but deep river was at our back, its vegetated and steep opposite bank only metres away, a perfect escape route should we need one. I felt confident about our situation, quite relaxed about it, until I looked at Ben's face that is.

I could never in truth say Ben had turned pale, but that was my first impression. His eyes had grown, no doubt about that. They were wide and bulging as though pressurised from behind, the whites standing out against the black of his skin. His nostrils were pinched and pale around the rims. His mouth downturned from its usual wide smile and his lips had lost colour. This was no act for my benefit. Ben was worried, no doubt about it.

In hushed whispers, we discussed our situation. One moment he wanted us to retrace our steps over already covered and known to be safe ground, safer than moving forwards into unknown territory. But that would mean travelling in the same direction as the elephants. We could wade the river but here it was deep, narrow and swift-flowing, a risk in itself. And the far bank was 'Turkana' territory and the Turkana were 'very bad people'. Ben couldn't decide the lesser of the two evils, ele or his bad neighbours the Turkana. Added to these concerns was his very obvious feeling of responsibility for my safety. I felt relaxed about the whole thing, not in any immediate danger, but then sometimes a little knowledge can be a dangerous thing. We opted to remain where we were and see how things developed.

The elephants moved on past, disappearing from view, their feeding noises fading with distance. We sat for a further five minutes in case of stragglers, before rising and continuing our cautious way along the river bank. Ben was now a bit more relaxed but still nervous about bumping into animals that may have chosen to follow the river rather than travel with the main herd. Progress was slow and the delay had cost us close to an hour.

As we increased distance from the danger so I could sense a difference in Ben's confidence. His back straightened, shoulders widened, his pace became smoother, more relaxed, the shotgun now held in one hand rather than at high-port across his chest.

Finally, we emerged from the bush into a village of about one hundred people, the ground bare and smooth, a variety of thatched or tin-roofed mud-walled huts scattered around a central well. One of the larger buildings doubled as a shop, its wooden shelving carrying bags of mealie flour, tins of curried vegetables, pilchards in tomato sauce, candles, matches, bottles of pop, paraffin, lots and lots of bags of sugar. It also had cigarettes. I bought two packs and Ben chatted with the lady owner. From his display, I got the impression he was describing our brush with the elephants and how only his remarkable bravery and cunning had saved the day.

We began our return walk, retracing our steps, and soon bumped into Jon coming up the river bank towards us. Our unexpected delay had worried him and he'd set out at speed to find us. When Ben mentioned the elephants as being the reason for our delay Jon said that yes, he too had seen them, considered them no threat and had walked on by. This is exactly what we did on our return journey, Jon in the lead.

It wasn't just elephants Ben was afraid of.

In one of our camps he hacked out a small open space for me to sleep in, about five metres from where he and Jon would lie by the fire. This was out of consideration, offering me my own little alcove. It was a warm, mosquito-free night and I slept with my sleeping bag open and down around my waist. Though on the equator the Laikipia area is at high elevation and temperatures drop overnight, especially during the last couple of hours before dawn. I woke about four in the morning, a frost-like chill in the air encouraging me to pull my bag up around my shoulders and revel in its warmth. Now wide awake I lay there and enjoyed the slow fading of the stars as the sky began to lighten. That's one of those facts that always tickles me. The stars are always there, we don't see them in daylight.

As I lay there I felt something move beneath my thick but lightweight foam mattress. This wasn't a gentle movement. This was a slow, powerful and purposeful movement and it went on for some moments. My mind immediately registered 'snake' and I did what all intrepid adventurers do in this kind of situation and froze solid, a more instinctive reaction than considered.

The movements slowed, stopped. A gentle twitch, a shuffle. The snake, and I was now sure it was a snake, had made itself comfortable beneath the small of my back, enjoying the heat transmitted through the foam mattress. How sweet, I didn't think.

I began to settle down, my heart rate returning to normal, and my brain beginning to function once more. The snake had stilled. It was comfortable, enjoying the warmth. There was a lot of material between it and me. It had no intentions of doing me harm, didn't know I existed as such, I was nothing more than a warm lump from which it could gain heat. All I had to do was rise, step out of my sleeping bag and walk away in my boxers.

Then what? My clothing was my pillow. My small rucksack lay nearby. I'd have to move the snake before I could retrieve these items, and my sleeping bag and mattress. I decided I'd wait until Ben and Jon woke up before I made my move. Safety in numbers and all that. They may well kill the snake with their kerries. Not that I wanted the snake dead. It hadn't done me any harm. Well, not yet it hadn't. I wanted Ben and Jon to see the snake I'd been sleeping on top of. This was not to boost my ego or present myself as some roughy toughy bush dweller who slept on top of venomous serpents as a matter of course. I wanted them present to witness it had happened and was not the figment of an over-active imagination. The fact is, the snake, if indeed there was a snake, was now so still and unobtrusive I was beginning to doubt its presence myself. I dozed, even slept for a while. This is common in some people when they suffer extremes of stress or feel in mortal danger. It's called fainting.

Though every morning I'd joined the others for early tea at the fire I knew this wasn't expected. Ben wanted to serve me my tea and biscuits in bed. It was one of the things he was there to do. I was the guest and he was there to look after me. Sometimes I felt I was denying him fulfilment by joining them at the fire. This particular morning, assisted by the thought the snake may still be snoozing away beneath me, I opted to let tea and biscuits come to me.

Ben arrived in my bushy little alcove beaming ear to ear. Finally, I was playing the white man and allowing him to fulfil his duties of being the person delegated to look after me and ensure I enjoyed myself. In one hand he carried an enamel mug of steaming tea, in the other two digestive biscuits. He looked like a kid on Christmas morning–until I told him there was a snake under my bedding. He halted, his look changing from one of joy to disbelief.

"No," he said.

"Yes," I replied.

"No," he said, a little less sure now, taking a step backwards.

"Oh yes," I said and with that rose from my bed.

I'd rehearsed this move several times in my head and when I executed it I have to admit things went with amazing smoothness. In one fluid movement I sat upright, bent my knees and moved onto my feet, standing up and allowing my nylon sleeping bag to slither down my body and pool around my ankles–rather in the same way I'd often imagined Michelle Pfeiffer removing her tight-fitting black cocktail dress before me. I then stepped from the sleeping bag in the same smooth style and stood, very un-Michelle Pfeiffer-like, in my boxers next to Ben.

For a moment we stood side by side looking down at my sleeping kit as though expecting something to happen, though I'm not sure what. As Ben had his hands full and wasn't taking the initiative I thought I would. Bending forwards I lifted the corner of the foam mattress, raising it higher and higher until the offending snake lay exposed. It was a puff adder, much smaller than it had felt. For a moment we stared at it and it stared back at us, no raising of its head, not even a flicker of the tongue. It was tempting to imagine it felt guilty, caught in the act like a kid with a hand in the cookie jar. But of course, it didn't. It remained still in the hope of going undetected, utter stillness being the best camouflage. And then all hell broke loose. Ben jumped backwards, a startled, fearful cry emitting from his throat, eyes wide and bulging white. My tea went over one shoulder, my biscuits over the other. Spinning on his feet Ben turned and ran back towards the safety of the fire and kitchen area.

Puff adders sometimes 'play dead'. (This is a handy tactic should you discover the pretty lady you've been chatting to is married to the psychopath glowering from the end of the bar). This snake chose not to. I'm sure that had it too been carrying tea and biscuits they would have been discarded in the same style Ben employed. No doubt frightened by Ben's sudden movement, in the blink of an eye it was gone, disappearing into the thick bush close by. I pulled on my shorts and T-shirt, stuck my feet into my boots, bundled my bedding and tucked the rest of my belongings under my arm. Picking up the abandoned enamel mug still hot from the memory of tea, I made my way to join the others. At least the snake hadn't been a figment of my imagination.

I'd slept on the ground many times before this event, and I've done so hundreds of times since. This is the only time I've experienced sharing my bed with a snake.

The only other snake encountered was quite a large one.

It was mid-morning, the sun already high, the day heating up. We walked in the usual order with Ben out in front towing the camels along, Jon walking behind the second camel, and me behind him. The path we followed was narrow with tall trees on our left and a gently sloping, vegetated bank dropping away on our right. Jon stopped, peered down the bank at something, took a step closer towards the edge then waved me up beside him. Beneath us and not more than five metres away lay a very large snake, the biggest I've seen before or since. It wasn't coiled but lay in short lengths, a kind of north/south, north/south arrangement, in the way boerewors are often laid out in rectangular polystyrene trays in supermarkets. I would guess it was four to five metres long and as thick as my thigh in its middle. I wasn't sure if it was sun-basking to gain body heat, digesting a meal (though there was no obvious bulge of swallowed prey), or playing dead in the hope we'd pass on by and leave it in peace. Its head was large, flat and coffin-shaped suggesting it was a python.

While all this was going through my mind Jon was shouting and gesticulating to Ben, encouraging him to come back and take a look at what we'd found. Frustrated by this delay Ben hobbled the lead camel and made his way back to us, shotgun rattling on his shoulder as it banged against his hip with each disgruntled step. As he drew near he looked at us both as if to say 'well, why have we stopped? What's all the fuss about?'

Trying hard to suppress his grin Jon indicated the snake with a professional flourish, like a magician producing a rabbit from a hat. Ben's mouth fell open and again I was impressed how his eyes seemed to grow in size, as though pressured from behind. Spinning on his feet like a ballet dancer he set off running back towards where the camels waited in abject boredom, flapping his arms and shouting 'bad snake!' bad snake!', desperate to get out of the area soonest and behaving as though the snake were in hot pursuit, which it wasn't. Jon looked at me, grinning ear to ear, delighted by his joke at Ben's expense. He shrugged, took one last look at the snake, then turned to follow the now disappearing Ben who was towing his bemused camels with renewed vigour into the distance.

Snakes are a hazard in Africa. It's estimated they are responsible for one thousand human deaths each year in Kenya and thirty thousand in sub-Saharan Africa. Often they are killed indiscriminately, more often in fields where people are working or when found close to settlements. Although this goes against the grain with me I do understand. It's removing a problem conclusively, in the same way you or I set a trap for a harmless mouse, or spray the bedroom for mosquitoes. In much of rural Africa the risk of envenomation is a major concern. Medical aid may be many hours, even days away, and few have access to transport.

On this trip, I was surprised the shotgun never came into play when snakes were encountered. Ben and Jon, their physical disadvantages leaving them unsuitable for most rural work, had been taken under the wing by John and his family from an early age. It could be an attitude of 'leave well alone' had been instilled.

There are several ways of going on a walking safari. One of these is to do as I did, with support from camels.

Ours were Dromedaries, the single-humped variety of camel. Introduced to Kenya by nomadic Somalia communities over one thousand years ago these animals are well suited to the arid conditions of the north. They are browsers more than grazers and have soft cushioned feet rather than hooves, these characteristics reduce environmental damage through over-grazing and soil disturbance. As well as being an excellent mode of transport, camels, like other domesticated livestock, are a source of meat, hides and milk. In conditions of drought, they continue to lactate long after cattle and goats have dried up.

The two camels accompanying us carried all we needed for almost a week in the bush, including water which is bulky and weighs a kilogram for every litre.

Their saddles were simple 'X' affairs, made on the farm. Wooden boxes containing food and cooking gear, or the jerry cans of water, were attached to each side. Softer, lighter items like bedrolls were strapped to the top. Though at times the animals whined and moaned like aged relatives during loading there was never any serious trouble with them. They enjoyed walking at their own casual, hypnotic pace and performed their tasks with aplomb, carrying their loads with a resigned but aristocratic air.

They drank only once on the trip, this when we camped close to a large waterhole allowing them to spend a relaxing afternoon standing knee-deep in muddy water browsing from shore-line trees. The only time they ate was between mid-afternoon and twilight when hobbled to prevent wandering they browsed as they wished. Ben told me they could go for five days without food or water.

As darkness approached Jon would bring them back to camp and command them down close by the fire. Moaning and groaning like a pair of disgruntled pensioners they would lower themselves to the ground, front first with legs folded on each side, then their back end, legs pointed forwards. A rope would be tied from before one front foot, passed over the top of the shoulders, then tied off above the other front foot, hobbling them by preventing them from rising. Some of you reading this may think that primitive and cruel but it was as much for the camel's benefit as for ours. Not only did it prevent them from rising and wandering off during the night but should predators appear it would stop them rushing off in panic into the unprotected darkness. Humans are not the only creatures on earth to understand the principle of 'divide and conquer'.

There was something very pleasing about walking with camels. It felt very natural, like things were meant to be. There was no 4WD mounted camp crew taking down one camp and then dashing ahead to set it all up again for that night. There was no burning of fossil fuels, no smell of diesel and exhaust, no intrusive engine noise and no two-tracks through the bush. We were quiet, slow, natural, using only already established game trails, taking nothing but our time and leaving nothing but camel dung. We were also completely self-sufficient, devoid of all technology, and there was a strange pleasure, a satisfaction in this. We could walk light and free, without the burden of a rucksack. Without the camels there to carry water the walk would have been impossible.

The camels had character, personalities of their own, and they were as much a part of the team as Ben, Jon or myself. The feeling we were working with nature, part of it rather than a temporary visitor like some mobile moviegoers, instilled feelings of greater intimacy with the bush.

I'd recommend a camel supported foot safari to anyone, yourself included.

As you get into the spirit of the venture and begin to feel familiar and comfortable with daily routines, the whole thing comes to an end.

We arrived back mid-afternoon and I accompanied John on a short trip to one of his stock posts before darkness fell. On our return we encountered a herd of elephants, sitting watching them as they grazed and browsed through the trees, bellies rumbling, calves playing and squealing and kicking up dust, a pleasant swan song to the venture.

I can't tell you much about my last evening in the company of John and Amanda because I don't remember too much about it. Friends of theirs arrived early, the beer and stories flowed, and my recollections are pleasant but hazy.

I left early the following morning and bumped and rattled and swerved my way back to Nairobi and the rental office in the Shell station, arriving a few hours before my flight out was due.

The first person I saw as I drove into the forecourt was the flower seller. He was dressed exactly as I'd last seen him, standing at the edge of the tarmac, a bunch of roses dark as red wine in his hand, a look of quiet expectation on his face. It was like a time warp and I did wonder if he'd been awaiting my return all that week, terrified to move in case he missed me.

I parked in a vacant bay, got out and stretched cramped muscles and pot-hole abused back, his eyes watching me all the while. I could feel them on me, an audience to my every move. I dragged my rucksack out, beat the dust from it, locked the vehicle up, my every action observed, his eyes all but boring into me, imploring me to make eye contact so he could smile as though in surprise and make his approach. In some ways I felt annoyed by this expectation, in other ways impressed by his tenacity and hopeful anticipation. Surely I wasn't the only good sales bet in Nairobi?

I began walking towards the rental office and he moved to intercept me, his demeanour humble, his face full of hope. A deal is a deal and I wasn't going to go back on my word though I had no need nor reason to buy roses. I didn't haggle but counted out his price from my remaining wad of crumpled and dusty Kenya shilling. I can't be sure if it was my lack of resistance or the fact I paid what he asked without argument, but as he handed me the roses and gazed in near disbelief at the crumpled notes he now held, he beamed from ear to ear and backed away nodding and bowing and repeating 'thank you, baas, thank you, baas'.

When I entered the office, rucksack in one hand, roses in the other, my friend the Sikh rolled his eyes with resignation.

He became a bit more animated and head bobbing when we inspected his Suzuki and other than the thick coating of dust he found it more or less as he'd released it. So pleased was he to have his vehicle returned without damage or the predations of nefarious criminals and corrupt police officers he allowed me the use of the staff shower then offered to drive me to the airport. We took the Suzuki of course, allowing him to test drive it before returning my deposit.

I was still stuck with a large and rather intrusive bunch of roses which I doubted would be welcome on my flight to South Africa. Wondering what I could do with them I came up with a cunning plan. As we negotiated the dodgem like traffic I asked my Sikh friend about his wife and his family. Like any proud husband and father, he was more than happy to elaborate. Between much swerving, horn usage, head bobbing and exquisitely worded doubts regarding other road users' pedigree, he told me of his four children. They were all well brought up, of most impeccable manners and high education, successful professionals with promising careers. He and his wife now lived a quiet but happy life alone. It transpired she was allergic to flowers. Cancel that brilliant idea then.

He dropped me off outside the terminal. With much head bobbing and shaking of hands we said our goodbyes and I made my way into the building. On the approach to the check-in desks stood a very dainty, very attractive Indian girl, dressed in a white blouse and neat suit as though for a business meeting. She held a handwritten sign saying 'Mister Colin'. I guessed that was me. With much smiling and bowing she positively gushed, handing me my tickets, apologising for not getting them to me earlier, and mentioning she'd interrupted her family's Sunday lunch to deliver them but this was of no consequence as it was a great pleasure to be of service. I thought it was more a case of 'services beyond the call of duty' and told her so.

Then I gave her the roses.

Death, Taxes, and Smoking Land Rovers

I have a Land Rover in Africa and for most of the time I'm there it's my home. It's a 1995 Defender 110 Tdi tin top with 3 doors and almost half a million kilometres on the clock.

It has wall-to-wall carpeting in the back, a full-length roof rack with an access ladder, auxiliary fuel and water tanks–all courtesy of the previous owner. Other than that it's pretty well standard which is how most vehicles should be.

I bought it for a song in KZN and drove it south to my sister's small farm in the Eastern Cape. It broke down twice on the way. I set about converting it from the dog kennel it had been for the previous couple of years into a vehicle that would carry me and my meagre belongings anywhere I wanted to go in Southern Africa–or beyond.

Since then I've depended on it for all my travels. It's taken me places I didn't believe a vehicle could go. It's provided shelter during storms and shade on blistering hot afternoons. It's been my kitchen, my bedroom, and on occasion my sitting room. It's given me mobility and safety. Since its very early days when it struggled to travel from the farm to East London without some minor–or major–hiccup, it's never let me down.

I'm not saying that since those early days it hasn't required work and expense, it has, and regularly. Considering what it's done, the places it's been and the conditions it's endured, this is more than acceptable. Any vehicle would need the same.

It's not pretty, it has its faults, and it has the aerodynamics of a brick, but the base vehicle originated in someone's back-garden shed in 1947, so none of this should be surprising. What does surprise and hearten is that a vehicle designed way back then is still seen in frequent use today, a credit to the vehicle, the designer, the manufacturer, and to those who still drive them.

Land Rovers, especially Defenders, seem to affect most people in one of two ways. They either love them or hate them. I would class myself somewhere between. I admire them and enjoy them. Most of all I like their honesty, their integrity. They might be basic, even antiquated in many respects, but they don't tell lies. They have no pretensions. They don't purport to be anything other than what they are. There are times I wonder if had I the means would I own something other than a rather beaten up Defender?

I was brought up with Land Rovers. I learned how to drive in a Land Rover. I even tried to take my driving test in a Land Rover, an idea rejected by my examiner. Part of the test involved leaving a kerb side on a steep hill using clutch and handbrake to ease the vehicle out from the parking spot while using the rearview mirror to ensure the coast was clear. This wasn't possible in a Land Rover unless you had a neck like a giraffe. Back then the handbrake lever was down at floor level next to your left heel. The rearview mirror was where rearview mirrors usually are, at the top centre of the windscreen. Try craning your neck to normal height when you're bent over looking at your feet.

I had a Land Rover of one sort or the other until 1978. When I went looking for a replacement there was none to be had. I bought a Subaru MV pickup. A year later I bought one of the first Toyota Hilux 4x4 models to enter the UK. It cost less than half that of a new Land Rover. In 1983 I bought another Hilux. Land Rovers were still hard to come by. The manufacturer that had opened up the world, be it Africa, the Middle East, Australia, New Zealand or South America, struggled to meet demand. The Japanese filled the void and have never looked back.

Here in Southern Africa, many people appear to find Land Rovers comical, a joke, even ridiculous. They are considered outdated, unreliable, sluggish and problematic. There is also–among certain factions who though not present during it appear to remember the Boer war quite well–a dislike for the vehicle because of nationality. Most of those holding these disparaging views drive recent model Land Cruisers–whether they can afford to or not.

On the opposing side of the fence sit the Land Rover enthusiasts who, well, enthuse about their chosen mode of transport. I won't deny that in comparison to more modern 4x4 vehicles Defenders are basic and like being rolled over and having their tummies tickled. Against that they are rugged, simple to maintain, easy to work on, and as time has proven they are durable and long-lived. They are also cheap on fuel. Parts for them can be found at a reasonable price in most places–quite often in the middle of nowhere. A lot of parts from one model will fit a different model, making them recyclable. They are very capable off-road. Even without the help of 'hill hold', 'decent control', 'front and rear locking differentials', 'variable throttle control' and all the other modern gizmos that remove skill and common sense from the job of driving in taxing conditions, they perform as well as every more modern vehicle I've driven–sometimes better.

I do wonder why Defenders raise such negative reactions among those who don't own one, and in most cases never have. I suspect it's jealousy, but not material jealousy. It's jealousy stemming from confidence and capability.

Many Defender owners have a good idea of how their vehicles work. They own basic toolkits and can fix minor problems at the side of the road. They tend to take pride in this and enjoy tinkering and understanding how their vehicle works. They are familiar with and know how to overcome the most common problems. Hat's off to them. I'd challenge many owners of more modern and complicated vehicles to do the same–assuming they know how to open the bonnet.

It's all very well to own a new or two or three-year-old and very capable 4x4 with all the modern amenities and comforts. It must be wonderful to set off up the motorway, cruising at 120kph, air con blasting, sound system singing, in car entertainment showing the latest movie. It must be confidence-inspiring to drive a state-of-the-art off-road vehicle allegedly capable of taking you deep into the bush where you can scratch your hairy chest, gaze at distant horizons with steely grey eyes, and generally conquer and dominate all–all that in truth frightens you. That's the rub. Most people who venture into it are frightened of the bush. They are frightened of not having a cold beer every night, frightened of not having air-con to keep them cool during the heat of the day, and frightened of not having fresh meat to throw on the braai every evening. They worry about their vehicles breaking down and stranding them miles from the nearest help, leaving them at the mercy of the elements, of nature and its wild creatures, of the dark. At the mercy of their inabilities.

Even more, they worry about their lack of knowledge and understanding being recognised. Nobody likes to look a fool. So they arm themselves with a vehicle as new as possible on the basis that the fewer kilometres it's done the less chance of it developing a problem. I can understand all that, even accept for most it's a sensible solution.

What I fail to understand is why those who choose this path and have the means to do so should then feel so superior to the humble Land Rover owner that every opportunity to deride and ridicule them is taken. I can only think these attitudes stem from feelings of imagined superiority–or concerned inferiority.

I admire Land Rover owners. There is a pride seldom recognised in owning one. In my case, it's inverted snobbery–and a lack of funds to buy anything better. With others, it can be anything from loyalty to the brand too wishing to drive the iconic safari vehicle, or having a vehicle you feel confident about fixing should things go wrong. And let's face facts, every vehicle can and often does go wrong, nothing is fool-proof and to convince yourself otherwise is to be an ostrich and stick your head beneath the sand.

Ostriches don't do that, they are not that stupid. This belief is based on their tendency to lie flat, their necks extended, heads pressed to the ground, when trying to conceal themselves, usually while sitting on the nest. Considering the generally open terrain they inhabit it seems an intelligent way of avoiding detection. Ostriches are–like other creatures sharing this planet with us–fascinating and brighter than we give them credit for.

Male plumage is black and white. Females are grey. They take turns incubating the eggs, the male during darkness, and the female during daylight. How sensible.

A mature male often has a small harem of females, but has one 'first wife'. She lays her eggs in the centre of the chosen nesting spot, usually nothing more than a hollow scraped out of the soil. The subordinate females then take their turns laying in the same nest–around the outside of the first wife's eggs. Should a mongoose or jackal come along and steal an egg it goes for those on the outside of the nest. The first wife's eggs are safe.

Ostriches are precocial. It's believed parents and chicks can bond–this by sound both ways–through the eggshell so the moment the chick emerges it knows who it's dealing with. Being precocial they are up and running in no time, feeding themselves and not relying on parents to bring food. The male and first wife look after the brood and it's not a good idea to get between parent and offspring. An acquaintance has an Isuzu pick-up truck that still bears battle scars from being kicked to hell and back by an irate male looking after chicks. This male dented and punctured the pick-up's bodywork in several places while the first wife herded the chicks out of danger.

Ostriches are almost as fascinating as Emus, but I'm not going to go into them here.

Back to Land Rovers, and their owners, another curious and interesting species.

My model has three bedrooms. The first is outside on the ground, when the weather is suitable and there are no predators in the area–sleeping head against a wheel, feet towards the fire. The roof rack sleeps two in comfort when the weather is dry and the stars to die for–and hyenas frequent the area. Finally, inside on the bed-board when rain threatens or mosquitos plague–and in areas where lions prowl at night. All three bedrooms have an ensuite bathroom–just choose your bush. It has hot and cold running water supplied from the 35-litre underwing tank. First thing in the morning it's cold when you'd like it to be warm. Late in the afternoon and early evening, after a day of blistering heat, it's hot when you'd like it to be cold.

I've already mentioned the wall-to-wall carpeting, courtesy of the one and only previous owner. I suspect his wife must have been quite fussy. This carpeting stinks something terrible, especially when it's damp. This has a lot to do with the fact the vehicle was as a dog kennel for two years before I came upon it, sitting rear door akimbo so the dogs could jump in and out whenever it suited them and shelter from the rain, or take a long snooze, as dogs like to do.

My Land Rover does have a few drawbacks. What vehicle doesn't?

It's noisy and it hates to cruise over 100kph. But where's the rush and who needs a radio? I don't. It doesn't have one anyway. And look on the bright side, it's unlikely I'll ever be done for speeding.

The instrument pod is stitched to the main dash with cable ties, all mountings having broken due to time and sunlight fatigued plastic.

The floor mats are industrial flooring rubber, the originals having decomposed like rotting logs.

When it rains my right knee gets soaked. It's like sitting under a tap, water pouring from the top front corner of the door. I need to fix that sometime but having spent much of my time living in the desert, rain is seldom a problem.

The steel firewall between the passenger compartment and engine bay is rotting away with rust, as are the steel box section door frames–all three of them.

The driver's door tends to open by itself when travelling over rough ground, then at other times refuses to open. All three door lock mechanisms frequently jam. Now and then the driver's side window falls like a brick down into the door, all by itself. When the once 3-speed heater fan, now a 1-speed unit, is switched on the cab begins to fill with exhaust fumes. Who needs a heater in the desert? And besides, I smoke so a bit of diesel exhaust is a welcome change–and it kills the permanent scent of wet dog.

And finally, talking of exhausts, my Defender does blow a head-turning puff of black smoke on start up. It's a feature of the model, so I'm assured. If nothing else this gets you noticed.

My Land Rover also has an auxiliary fuel tank built in. This increases its capacity to 115 litres giving it a range of well over 1,000 kilometres under all but the most demanding conditions. In deep, soft, sand fuel consumption goes up about 20%.

Overall consumption is around 10km/L, this from an engine first designed and built almost 30 years ago, an engine without all the electronic gizmos and recycling systems mandatory today to reduce both fuel consumption and exhaust emissions. Over the past few years, due to work situations, I've driven several Toyota Land Cruisers. These 'modern' vehicles seldom return as high as 5km/L.

As mentioned before, the downside of owning a Land Rover, especially in southern Africa, is the uninvited flack you often endure. Many consider themselves entitled to comment on, even criticise, another person's life choices. I do struggle with this one and in the main let these comments wash over without offering defence or argument. What's the point? Everyone is entitled to their opinions. Sadly few realise their opinions are just that–theirs, and simply opinions.

But there is a light-hearted side to all this and I enjoy this kind of flack if only because it brings a smile.

Over here, as in most countries, Land Rover Defender owners wave and flash their lights at one another when they meet on the road, whether they know one another or not.

You may think this strange. It is. I find it strange yet I'm now into the habit myself. Subaru or Ford or Nissan owners don't wave and flash at total strangers because they are driving the same make of vehicle, so why the hell do Defender drivers do so?

It may be because we are a persecuted minority, deemed a joke by many of the 4x4 fraternity. We are outlaws, lepers, comedians, idiots ... call us what you will but that's how it often feels owning a Land Rover. You're an oddity, there is something wrong with you, a deficiency between the ears.

So we band together, rejoice when we see another of the same ilk, someone who understands us as we understand them. We are part of a clan and our badge, our uniform, and the way we recognise one another is the vehicle we drive.

In the very early days, when my Land Rover struggled to travel from the farm to East London without at least one halt each way where it would sit panting at the side of the road while I tinkered and twiddled and tickled its tummy, even Lindsey, my sister, thought I'd lost the plot. Finally, after a troublesome couple of months and quite a bit of work and knowledge building, I felt confident enough to take my Land Rover on its first proper road trip, a kind of trial run before heading north through the wilds of Botswana where the only help I could expect in most places would be my own.

Lindsey opted to come along with me, get some time off the farm and from behind the kitchen sink. We would spend two weeks traversing the Karoo. Vehicle loaded with basic camping equipment off we set.

About an hour into the trip we met another Land Rover coming from the opposite direction. Headlamps flashed and hands waved with excitement from behind windscreens. I returned the greetings. Lindsey looked at me, saying nothing, her expression asking if I knew these people. I shrugged. I was already familiar with this rather strange behaviour and understood it. I wasn't going to explain. Besides, my Land Rover is so noisy conversation is difficult unless you enjoy shouting.

Another hour, another Land Rover, the whole process repeated. After they had passed I looked at Lindsey. She looked at me. Again her expression queried if I knew those people and if so how. I didn't comment.

And then a third one appeared. Again the lights began to flash, this time from far out.

"Oh look!" commented Lindsey, pointing at the oncoming vehicle. "Another masochist."

Thanks, sis.

Several years ago, having had the black hand of Africa yet again thrust firmly in my face, I left Namibia and bolted for the Botswana border. A couple of days later I sat nursing a beer in the bar of the Old Bridge in Maun, wondering what the hell I was going to do with myself now. It was the off-season, there was no work on offer at such short notice, and I had little money. What I did have was my Land Rover, enough cash to kick about for at least a couple of weeks and pay for food and fuel until I got back into South Africa.

I opted to travel down through the Central Kalahari Game Reserve, a genuine wilderness about the size of Wales and almost devoid of people. It would be quite an undertaking. I didn't have internet but I did have friends from previous visits to Bots who would provide valuable knowledge and advice about my proposed trip. One of these mates was Crispen, a man with an interesting background, a very short fuse, and a workshop in Maun where he deals with Land Rover and Toyota safari vehicles. We met in the bar of the Old Bridge and enjoyed a few beers while I picked his brain about the best routes and anticipated fuel requirements. He's spent a lot of time in the CKGR and knows it well. His main concern was–rather touchingly for Crispen–my safety. Most of those who attempt this trip do it in convoys of three vehicles. I would be doing it solo.

It's about 250 km from Maun to Rakops, the last place you can pick up fuel before entering the CKGR. Crispen asked if that was the route I was taking and I told him it was. I would fuel up at Rakops and then enter the reserve by the NE gate at Matswere.

"You still driving the same old Land Rover?" Crispen asked.

"Yea, for sure, the same one," I replied with a touch of perverse pride.

"Oh, ok. No need to worry about your safety then mate. You won't even make it to the fuel station in Rakops."

Thanks, Crispen.

I hinted earlier that had I the means I may be driving something different. I'm not sure if that's true. I do on occasion suffer Land Rover envy when I see others driving late model Defenders with gleaming paintwork and doors that close. But I like my Land Rover, it has personality, character, it has soul. Yes, it does have its drawbacks and it does have niggling problems. And yes, I've taken a lot of stick over the years for being a Land Rover owner. But the vehicle 'fits', both me and the work I expect it to do. It's also one of my ways of waving two fingers at the rest of the world and saying 'bugger you, I don't care what you think, I'm happy'. And I am. I'm very, very happy with my rather tatty and bedraggled old lady. She's a gem. What's more, I believe she'll still be around when Land Cruisers, Patrols, Jeep Cherokees, Hi-lux and all the rest of them half her age are on the scrap heap. In a world of built-in obsolescence and gross over-consumption, you can't say much better than that.

Karma hey! She's a Bitch Sometimes

I don't like guidebooks. Or should I say I don't like using guidebooks. I do understand why so many others find them invaluable, especially those on tight schedules or travelling without pre-booked accommodation. But for me, they don't work and I'm not sure why. Maybe I don't want to be where everyone else is. Maybe I'm happy not having a clue where I'm going.

On my first visit to South Island New Zealand I was (and still am) stunned by the scenery. It was Scotland on steroids, only–dare I say it–more beautiful to my eye. I could sit and drink in the same basic view for hour after hour, watching the changing picture as cloud shadows drifted across mountainsides, or cats-paws of wind spread like spilt oil over the surface of a lake, distorting the near-perfect reflections of backdrop. It was never boring and my eyes and mind revelled in the changing beauty of the landscape. I had little need for anything other than this. It was the country and how it functioned I'd come to see and indulge myself in. But each to their own and we are all different.

Once, while sitting enjoying an early morning coffee on the Wanaka lakefront, looking out over the mirrored surface of water with those stunning mountains in the background, a small group of Japanese tourists took the table next to me. They ordered in seconds with scant regard to menu, their every action suggesting a need for speed, they were on a mission. While they waited for breakfast to arrive guidebooks were produced and pored over. A bright yellow high-lighter appeared and marked several points of interest I imagined they wanted to visit that day. When the count went over ten I began to squirm with discomfort. How in the hell did they hope to see, or enjoy, all those things in one day? Their food arrived, heads bowed and the table became silent as they ate in rushed dedication. The bill was paid before they'd finished. Mouths were wiped, napkins crumpled and discarded, last gulps from coffee cups taken as they pushed their chairs back. As one, like a school of fish or an evening flock of starlings, they rose and left. I don't think one of them had noticed, let alone taken in, the view before them as they sat eating breakfast. The function was to eat and get breakfast out of the way as soon as possible so they could drive off to other places where the function was to absorb the view rather than eat. I was still on my first cup of coffee.

I was bemused. I tried hard not to judge because they didn't do things in the same way I chose to do them. What bothered me was that back then, pre Lord of the Rings mania, most people visited New Zealand for extreme sports or extreme scenery. Anyone who has been to Wanaka or Te-Anu in the right weather will know how stunning the views can be. To sit enjoying an early morning coffee while absorbing those views is a veritable pleasure, heaven on earth. I can only guess that back then this was not a guidebook suggestion. If it's not in the guide book it's not worthy of attention.

Having said all that, years later, again on the South Island of New Zealand, I got an inkling why some are less fortunate than myself and have to cram everything in. At the Mount Cook centre there are coin-operated showers for day visitors. I was living out of the back of a car as usual and decided to take the opportunity when it was available. There was a queue and while sitting in the sunshine, awaiting my turn, I struck up a conversation with the Japanese lady sitting next to me. She was exhausted, felt grubby, and was very much looking forward to her shower. She was travelling with two other family members in a small rented motor home. They had only ten days holiday and hoped to travel all the North and South Island in that time, each taking spells at the wheel. It was all the time they could afford to take from work. No wonder she appeared exhausted.

But back to guide books. There are lots of good, sound reasons for using them, they just don't work for me. Often I've stumbled upon the most interesting, fulfilling and stimulating places while exploring. Other like-minded travellers–after careful consideration–might suggest a place of interest. These places are seldom given mention in the guidebooks. Long may that continue.

I do carry a guidebook in my Land Rover. It's about twenty years out of date and as it covers South Africa, Namibia and Botswana it's not exactly comprehensive. I've used it a couple of times when the small street maps of towns have helped me orientate myself in unfamiliar surroundings.

During a trip up through Botswana with LC, my partner at the time, this guidebook played a dubious role in assisting us find Tsodilo Hills. Spending a full day trying to find the only three hills in a vast area of otherwise flat Kalahari scrub may sound laughable, and it is. I am as much to blame for this travesty of navigation as LC. What makes all this worse is that I'd been there previously, well before the place became the tourist Mecca it now appears to be. Back then I was travelling by myself, using a map and what little common sense I possess. I found the place without any hassles and ended up the only camper staying on the vast community campsite close to the hills. I spent a fascinating three days, guided around the all-but empty site by a very informative San girl. At times it felt as though we were the only people there and I suspect this was true. As a finale, I climbed 'Male Hill' with my guide's elderly but very fit father, a man who professed to have been Sir Laurens Van Der Post's guide back in 1957. I have no reason to disbelieve him.

Tsodilo Hills, now a WHS (World Heritage Site), should stand out like sore thumbs in the middle of the smooth green felt of a billiard table. They do, but only when you get close up to them. One of the reasons I was keen to visit them was because they were the only hills for as far as the eye can see and further, quartzite intrusions rising above the flat surface of a fossilised lake and rolling Kalahari dunes. What an aberration.

Another reason for interest was antiquity, human rather than geographic antiquity. The San, believed to be our oldest ancestors, place huge cultural significance on Tsodilo Hills which they consider the birthplace of all life. The hills may have been inhabited for 100,000 years, from stone-age times until the present, and they contain around 400 rock art sites recording some of this history. I won't pretend I'm any kind of authority on these matters, I'm not. And I'm no culture vulture dashing from historic site to historic site snapping pictures and gleaning facts. For me, there is something moving in some sites of antiquity, a thread with the past. I've felt this most often when I've found discarded arrowheads and chips of flint. Picking them up, holding that small piece of rock which may well not have felt the dry touch of human fingers for hundreds of years, seems to melt and compress time, bring the past closer and make it tangible. Sometimes it's as though that touch allows me to sense the presence of our ancestors, fanciful though that may sound.

But of course, before you can ever experience any of these strange sensations of the past you have to get to the point of interest.

On this trip, LC and I left Maun with water and fuel tanks brimmed. Our ice box was stuffed with fresh foods which we hoped would last us five days, about the same time as the ice would keep. One of LC's last purchases was a large bag of crisp, green apples, something she had a penchant for, especially when dipped in peanut butter. The problem was she enjoyed her apples cold and insisted on keeping them in the limited space of our ice box. Not only did these apples compete with our other fresh foods of meat, boerewors, tomatoes etc., but they also competed for space with my beers. This, at times, proved a sore point. LC has red hair, flame red, and often displays the temperament associated with this fiery colour. We never came to blows and seldom raised our voices about what got priority in the limited space available in our ice box once the necessities were in, but it wasn't unusual to find beers removed to make space for apples, or vice-versa. On this trip, I was a touch 'nose-out-of-joint' to discover my six-pack of beers replaced by one beer and a large bag of apples. There was little point in becoming upset about this change of affairs, at least I'd still have one cold beer of an evening. I didn't even make mention of it.

Departing Maun mid-morning we headed southwest, turning north at Sehithwa and curving around the west side of the Okavango Delta. That first night we camped on the banks of the panhandle, a long slow deep sand drive from the sealed road but well worth the time and effort. When conditions are right the sunrise over the waters of the wide river and lagoons is breathtaking, the most spectacular and colourful I've seen. It's like looking at the world through rose-tinted filters. I wanted LC to enjoy these splendours and see for herself how the rising sun can make even the banks of tall, green reeds glow as though on fire, the slow-flowing waters go through several shades of mauve.

The following morning, having negotiated our way past a large convoy of South African 4WD's all stuck in the sand track and had our offers of assistance quite abruptly turned down, we regained the sealed road heading north, re-inflated our tyres, and began looking for the track heading west that would take us to Tsodilo Hills. That's where it all began to go a bit pear-shaped.

LC had found my ancient guidebook and decided to use this as the definitive source to take us to our destination. When I say ancient I do mean ancient. It was probably used by the Dorslandtrekkers on their trek from the Free State to Angola in 1870. It suggested we take the first, or most southerly, of three roads all heading west and converging on Tsodilo Hills. When LC mentioned this I disagreed. Gut feeling and vague memory told me that on my previous trip I'd opted for the second or central of the three optioned tracks. I was sure my now long disintegrated map had shown this track as a solid line whereas those north and south of it were lesser tracks. LC wasn't having any of it. She was on the maps that day, she'd call the shots.

As I drove, concentrating on the road ahead, she dug out her cell phone and activated the GPS. Another five minutes and she asked me to slow and look out for a track on our left. It was the one we wanted to take. A minute later it appeared and I nosed the Land Rover into it, then stopped. To me, it was obvious this was not the track we wanted. It was overgrown and the deep ruts in the sand hadn't seen wheels for a long time. 'Disused' was the word that sprang to mind. I looked at LC, my face expressing blank disbelief. She looked back at me with one of her 'Well, told you so' looks.

"This isn't it. Can't be. It's completely overgrown. Hasn't seen use for ages."

LC held up the guidebook, page open to show the line drawing map, finger pointing at the GPS coordinates for the start of the track. Then she held up her phone, the screen showing those same coordinates. I knew I was onto a loser. Before I met LC I'd often considered myself to be the most awkward, stubborn and bloody-minded person walking the planet. Now I knew better. I decided to use logic rather than argue.

"Look LC, it's a long time since I was here and back then the place was seldom visited. But even then the track was more obvious and more used than this one. This one is overgrown and unused. Tsodilo Hills is now a World Heritage Site, a bit of a tourist Mecca. There will be self-drive 4x4s and safari vehicles ... there might even be bloody great coaches going in and out regularly. There's not even a sign here suggesting this is the correct route."

LC's face set in full stubborn mode and she once more tapped the GPS coordinates on her phone's screen. In her book, this was an indisputable fact we were in the right place. I kept my cool. There was little point in becoming excited by any of this.

"All that proves is that we are in the correct spot for what once WAS the main track going to Tsodilo Hills, but look at it now! Does that look like a well-travelled track to you?" I said, finger-pointing out the windscreen at the remnants of the old two-track disappearing into overhanging vegetation.

LC didn't even bother looking but once more tapped her phone's screen, her face set in an expression of smug victory.

"Oh come on LC, look at it and tell me you believe that's a well-used track."

Still she refused to look through the windscreen.

"Do I tell you where to go when it's you who's on the maps?" she asked.

"No, but there's seldom any need to."

LC pursed her lips and narrowed her eyes. I got the message.

'What's the point' I thought. All we were going to do was argue. I was old-school and tended to question everything, relying on logic and limited common sense in most situations. LC was new-school and tended to do whatever modern technology told her to do, often without question. She was as stubborn as I could be and we could butt heads for hours, neither of us giving way. I looked at the vague memory of a track that lay before us. We weren't in any rush. I had faith in the Land Rover's abilities. If things became serious we could always turn around. It would be a bit of an adventure. Why not? It was better than arguing. And who knows, after a kilometre or so the track might open up, become firmer, I told myself, ever the optimist destined for constant disappointment. I got out of the Land Rover and deflated the tyres. I had a feeling this might turn out to be a very long day.

Half an hour later we were grinding through thick, soft sand in first gear, branches scraping down both sides of the vehicle like nails on a blackboard. I began to see the funny side of things.

"Nice track, hey LC! Surprised we haven't seen any other vehicles yet. It is a WHS we're going to, isn't it?"

LC ignored me, treating my taunts with the disdain they deserved. Now and then we'd both lean inwards, heads almost touching above the central console as we pushed through thorn trees, their springy branches whipping in through the side windows as we passed.

"Jeez, you'd think they'd do a bit of maintenance on the main track to a WHS, wouldn't you!" I'd exclaim.

"As you've so often pointed out, this is Africa," retorted LC, her tone suggesting she was becoming a little pissed off with my constant teasing.

And then we did meet another vehicle, travelling in the opposite direction to ourselves. It wasn't a tour bus or a safari vehicle. It wasn't even a self-drive 4x4. It was a donkey cart. Home built with a single axle and leaf springs, powered by two blinkered donkeys and piloted by a local man and his young daughter. It was loaded with Mopani wood to be sold out on the main road. One of the tyres was flat as a pancake, and the cart parked off the side of the track and going nowhere until this problem was fixed. The father and daughter were delighted to see us. Parking close I dug my compressor out of the back of the Land Rover and inflated both of the cart's tyres. As I did this I chatted with the father as best I could. Finally, as I packed the compressor away, I asked him if we were on the right road for Tsodilo Hills. His previously happy face lost all animation and he dropped his eyes. One of the difficulties often encountered in rural Africa is that people, especially those you've assisted in some way, never want to tell you what they feel you don't want to hear. It's not being dishonest as such. They don't want to be the bearers of bad news, don't want to be the ones to spoil your day, and they don't want to disappoint. Often they will tell you what they think you want to hear rather than tell you the unfortunate truth. For long moments there was silence and my new friend didn't want to make eye contact with me. I asked the question again, re-phrasing it.

"Does this road go to Tsodilo Hills?"

Finally he looked up and I could tell by his expression he was torn, wanting to tell the truth but not wanting to disappoint.

"Yes," he said, then added, "but there is another road."

Ah hah! I thought. Of course there is another road, and why mention it if it's not a better one. I encouraged and he gave details. If we returned to the main road and headed north for ten kilometres we'd find another road, a big road, a wide road, a good road. That was the road we wanted. I thanked him for his advice, for his honesty, and his smile returned. Then, ensuring LC was in earshot and listening, I asked him to once more confirm that the road we were on did go to Tsodilo Hills. His face fell. After a moment he rallied and told me that yes it did, but it had not been used for a very long time. He once again mentioned there was a good road, a wide road, a few kilometres further north. This confirmed it in my mind. The road we were on was not the one we wanted to be on.

Our new friend and his daughter climbed back onto their cart, urged the donkeys to walk and with much waving and smiles resumed their journey.

I looked at LC. Her face was set with determination.

"Well?" I asked.

"You heard him as well as I did," she replied, climbing into the Land Rover, "this road goes to Tsodilo Hills," and with that, she slammed the door.

For the next four hours we ground and churned and lumbered our way westward. Branches scraped down the wings or bent backwards against the screen pillars before flicking viciously through the side windows forcing us to lean hard over towards the centre of the car to avoid them. In long sections the sand was so soft and deep I'd have to select low ratio rather than strain engine and clutch. Now and then the track would disappear completely and rather than push blindly onwards I'd stop and get out, walking a large semi-circle in front of the vehicle and increasing its range with each sweep until once more the vague two-track became discernible.

We moved from Mopani woodland with sand substrate into an area dominated by thorn, the ground firmer and rock-strewn. Soon after we crested a low rise to find a settlement of scattered huts in the surrounding woodlands. The track led to the settlement water-point, a wind-operated pump taking water from a borehole to fill a couple of plastic tanks for human use. The overflow from these tanks spilt into a large, circular, cement-walled dam from which the livestock could drink. There were two horses and three cows drinking from the far side of this dam and as we approached they all stopped and looked up. Horses tend to be flightier than cattle and as we drew closer I could tell they were nervous about us. They stood motionless, water still dripping from black velvet muzzles, eyes wide and wary with the whites now visible. Their ears twitched back and forth with alarm at each change of engine noise or when a stone clanged and rattled beneath a wheel. I slowed to a crawl and angled my approach so as not to alarm them, but it was pointless. Even the cows regarded us with wary suspicion now. Seconds later, as one, the horses took a step backwards, heads thrown up, ears erect and eyes wide. In a flash they turned, their heads dropped on extended necks, and with a clattering of stones they galloped off into the trees without a backward glance. The cows wheeled and followed suit at a more sedate, high-stepping pace. We continued our slow trundle over the rock-strewn ground, the Land Rover pointing towards where I could see the track continuing on the far side of the stock dam. LC looked across at me. She'd seen plenty of livestock at water points before, but never any that reacted in the way these animals had.

"What made them run like that?" she asked.

"Guess they've never seen a vehicle before," I replied.

LC raised a curled fist, middle finger extended.

Soon after that one tiny settlement we were back into thick bush once more, the surface turning to sand again, the track even more overgrown than before. It occurred to me that the first section, from the main road to the settlement, though barely used, may have seen more traffic than the section we were now on. This belief strengthened over the next couple of hours as bit by bit the track deteriorated and became harder to follow. That's not to say it hadn't seen use, it had, in places quite heavily, but not by cars. It had been used by elephants, which, like humans and most other animals, find it much easier to trundle through the bush following an open path rather than pushing and weaving their way through thick vegetation and over rocks and fallen branches. Another thing elephants like to do as they wander along is push trees over, allowing them easy access to tender upper vegetation and the bark which they love to strip from boughs. Considering they are following the track as they browse along it's not surprising some of these pushed-over trees fall across it, effectively blocking it. The ele's had been quite busy along one section we followed. Several times we had to stop and remove smaller trees blocking our progress. There was also the debris of larger branches and the deep holes left in the sand by ele's that had gathered to enjoy some particularly tasty or succulent piece of greenery. Some of the fallen trees were too large for us to manhandle and we'd either have to tow them out of the way with the Land Rover or find a way around them.

The sun was high now, the temperature hot with no breeze in the low forest. Heat came through the glass of the windshield so it was like sitting in a greenhouse. Hot air wafted through the open windows bringing in clouds of the tiny Mopani bees which scrabbled and tickled over our faces in their delight of finding moisture in the corners of our eyes, up our nostrils, even deep in our ears. The metal floor and transmission tunnel of the Land Rover were too hot to touch and I could feel the accumulated heat of many hours of hard work seeping from the pedals through the soles of my boots. Dust and grit clung to sweat-soaked skins and clothing, crunched between our teeth and clogged the damp corners of our eyes. It would have been easy for LC and I to have a major fallout under these circumstances. Amazingly we didn't. In truth, I was rather enjoying the challenge, resigned to things as they were rather than dwelling on how they could have been. What should have been a cool and breezy drive on a decent gravel road had become an endurance trial and adventure, for us and the poor old Land Rover. It was another day in out-back Africa and I was enjoying the challenges it presented. Even more, I was enjoying LC's now obvious discomfort. Gone was the know-it-all obstinacy, even she realised it unlikely the main road to a WHS would be a tiny, narrow two-track blocked by fallen trees pushed over by wandering elephants. Not a lot was said and I refrained from rubbing things in though there were many times I was tempted. LC compensated for her error by assisting with every bough and tree that had to be removed and by helping to clear new paths around those we couldn't shift. She sweated and got dusty and thorn scratched and torn alongside me, never complaining, and never apologising other than through her efforts and actions. Can't say fairer than that.

It took us a long time to get through the area the ele's had crossed and no sooner had we done so than an even greater challenge presented itself.

The area we were travelling through was generally flat and featureless, the track itself offering a water course during the wet season. The soil was a mix of clay and sand and over the years, during spells of heavy rain, gulley erosion had begun, extending itself with every passing wet season. Several hundred metres of track and a wide area on either side of it had disappeared. What remained was impassable with some gullies so deep, wide and sheer-sided they would have swallowed the Land Rover, never to be seen again. The place reminded me of a battlefield that had suffered severe shelling. Even most of the vegetation had gone.

It was early afternoon and there was no way I was going to turn around and head back to the main road all those gruelling hours away, not if I could find an alternative.

We got out of the Land Rover and began to walk around the eroded area, assessing things as we went. Finally, we chose a route and began clearing it as best we could. I was leery about getting too close to any eroded area as often the water has eaten away well below the surface, showing no sign of collapse until you try to cross it with a heavy vehicle. One of the golden rules when travelling in the bush or out-back is that should things go a bit pear-shaped never, ever leave your vehicle. Not only will it provide shade and shelter it will also protect you from wild animals. If well stocked it will hold more food and water than you could ever carry. Most importantly it will be much more visible to search parties than you would be on foot. Much of my caution about the situation we found ourselves in stemmed from the fact that should the Land Rover fall into one of those gullies, or have the ground collapse beneath it, then it would be all but impossible to extract, not much use or useable as a shelter, and be hard to spot even from the air. Not that anyone was likely to come looking for us anyway. We hadn't informed anyone of our plans and no one could ever guess where we were. Even we could only say we were on a disused sand track somewhere in the northwest of Botswana, quite close to Tsodilo Hills. There is a vast amount of empty country out there and as LC confirmed, not much of it has cell phone coverage. But apart from all that, my only real concern was losing the Land Rover. If the shit did hit the fan then I was confident it was less than a day's walk back to the remote settlement we'd passed through. The real worry was that extracting and recovering a vehicle from a deep hole in the middle of nowhere would have cost more than the car was worth or I could afford.

An hour or so later we'd cleared a long curving track that I hoped would take us around the eroded area. LC walked in front, I crawled along in low ratio behind her. At least if the Land Rover did fall into a hole there would only be one of us trapped in it. It didn't and ten minutes later we emerged from the bush and back onto a discernible track.

As mentioned before, the area we traversed was like much of Botswana, flat and featureless, a vast, green sea of bush. At ground level the thick vegetation restricts vision and without distant landmarks it's hard to know where you are or where you're going. I'd been keeping an eye on the sun all day and was confident we'd been travelling west most of the time, roughly the direction we wanted to be going. Soon after rejoining the track after bypassing the erosion gullies, I felt we were heading southwards. This was confirmed when I stopped and checked with a hand-held compass. Bugger, now what! We must have missed a track taking us west and were now headed towards the middle of nowhere.

We backtracked, returning to the eroded area but without finding a track to take us more to the west. There was little option other than to continue on the southward heading track we were now on and hope that soon it would swing back towards the west.

Another twenty minutes of cautious driving and we emerged from the thorn thickets into an open area of bare sand. It was a remote farm post, stuck out miles from anywhere. There was a large goat kraal and not far behind it a low-roofed house made from the usual Mopani poles and corrugated steel sheeting. Dogs rose from the sparse shade cast by thorn trees and came to investigate. They were curious but not alarmed, only a couple of them offering to bark and I wondered if this was because they were unfamiliar with vehicles. When I stepped from the Land Rover a couple of them jumped back in alarm, skulking off with tails between their legs and hurried looks over their shoulders. If dogs can display a look of complete disbelief then a couple more of them did this but stood their ground as I approached. I stopped a couple of metres from them to allow them to come to me if they wished. There were none of the usual raucous rabbles of farm dogs with those in front of you barking and holding your attention while those behind you sneak in to bite. These dogs were wary but fascinated and it dawned on me why. They'd never seen white skin before. This was confirmed moments later as I stood and allowed them to come close and sniff at me, necks extended, eyes watching my face, ears twitching to the quiet but unfamiliar words I spoke. A man appeared from the shaded doorway of the hut and shouted at the dogs. They paid little attention until he stepped from the shadows and came striding towards us, the dogs scattering at his approach. He was about my height but powerful in build, blood vessels standing out cord-like over bulging biceps and thick forearms. Grey smoked through the hair at his temples and he dressed in the new traditional costume of a ragged T-shirt and baggy jeans. Between shouts at the still circling dogs he said something in Setswana to me.

"I'm sorry. I speak only English," I replied as we shook hands. He beamed with delight.

"Oh, Englaise! Welcome!" and he shook my hand even more vigorously as though I were his salvation rather than him being mine.

"I am sorry for dogs," he said, still shaking my hand and kicking out at the animals which were once more giving in to their curiosity and edging closer. "They never see a white person before."

For a minute or two we followed local custom of asking about one another's health and general happiness, discussed the weather and chatted about the goat market and the hazards of stock farming in an area where wild animals still abounded. As we went through these formalities I noticed another man, sitting on an old plastic picnic chair in the shade of a camel thorn. He'd been sowing a pair of jeans, patching them, but now he sat with hands stilled, mouth agape, as fascinated as his dogs by this unusual apparition in white.

Introductions over I explained our predicament and asked if he could offer directions to Tsodilo Hills. This was no problem he explained. We must have missed the track taking us west some kilometres back, then added no one used it these days anyway. It was prone to erosion and had suffered much damage over the past few years. His English was excellent which was fortunate as I speak no Setswana, and I wondered where he'd learned this, especially as he was now living in an area where this ability would be wasted. There was a moment's silence as I was thinking this and I guessed he was wondering himself, wondering why the hell we'd been using a track that no longer existed. I didn't bother trying to explain.

He began to give loose directions then must have decided I was so incompetent I'd never find the correct track without help. He offered to guide us there himself and ignored my assurances we'd be ok without him.

So off we set, our new friend and guide refusing to take a seat in the Land Rover and instead standing on the driver's side foot rail, hands holding onto the roof rack. The track we took was no better than any other track we'd used that day. Soft, deep Kalahari sand weaving between Mopani and thorn trees. Several times I had to put LC's side of the vehicle well off the road and into the bush to prevent our guide from being knocked off his perch by trees growing at the very edge of the track.

After four or five kilometres we came to another track. He told me to halt and explained if we turned left here we'd be heading towards Tsodilo Hills once again. Through a clearing in the vegetation, we caught our first sight of the hills themselves, rising above the woodlands about twenty kilometres from where we were. It was a pleasant shock to finally see them and now we were close they appeared so obvious I wondered why we hadn't noticed them before. A simple matter of angle and density of vegetation I guessed.

Our guide dismounted and pointed out the hills for us, grinning ear to ear, delighted by our obvious relief.

"Jump back on and I'll give you a lift back to your farm," I offered.

"No, no. I will walk back," he replied.

I tried to persuade him to accept a lift but he was adamant we should continue, explaining the track we were now on would swing well to the south of the hills before curving round and bringing us up on the far side of them. It was at least another hour's driving and the track would be hard to follow as darkness fell. Finally I agreed but wanted to offer him something for his generous assistance. I picked up a recently opened pack of cigarettes and offered it to him.

"Do you smoke?" I asked.

Amazingly he didn't. I thought everyone in Africa smoked, or at least knew someone who did. Cigarettes are generally prized and I'd never had their offer refused before. I climbed from the Land Rover, determined to repay him in some way though he insisted it wasn't necessary, he'd been happy to help. I led him round to the back of the vehicle, opened the rear door and dug into the ice box. I found what I was looking for immediately. LC's bag of apples of which she'd eaten only two.

"Do you like apples?" I asked, holding up the clear cellophane bag which still contained at least a dozen small, firm, juicy, green or yellow orbs. His face lit up, eyes wide with pleasure. Fresh fruit was an unheard of luxury in the middle of the Kalahari bush, at least one hundred kilometres from the nearest outlet. I thrust the bag into his hands and closed the Land Rover's door.

"Thank you, thank you," he stammered, quite overwhelmed by this gift but now prepared to accept it.

He stood and waved us goodbye as we turned onto this new track and vanished into the bush.

"Did you give him the whole bag?" LC asked.

"Fraid so."

"Oh ..."

As the sun dipped out of sight and darkness began to fall we arrived at the airfield. Yes, airfield. A small landing strip hacked from the native bush and levelled, all ant-bear holes filled in. But an airfield nonetheless, complete with windsock hanging limp in the breezeless evening air.

Soon after we crossed a well-graded road of white calcrete, wide enough to take two passing coaches with ease. This was the road we should have taken and it was the one we used to depart Tsodilo Hills four days later. Our outward trip took a little over an hour. It had taken us over nine hours to get in and cost LC a bag of treasured apples.

Karma hey!

Lost in Translation

It sounds obvious I know, but Africa is different. Africa is Africa, it's not Europe or North America, or anywhere else for that matter. Don't expect it to be like home, wherever that may be.

In the past I've been asked what are the most important things to take along on a trip to Africa. My advice is always the same. Take an open mind, a big smile, and a lot of patience.

There are all kinds of hurdles to overcome and if you are visiting without a guide you're going to have to jump them by yourself. The best advice I can offer is to keep smiling and try hard to understand the other person's perspective.

I'll offer a couple of examples from personal experience. Keep in mind that when these events took place I was more touched with sympathy and understanding tinged with gentle amusement, than with anger or frustration.

Water is scarce in much of Africa. Clean water, drinkable water, even more so. Bottled water costs. To make clean drinking water a more accessible commodity some supermarkets opted to produce their own. They now offer chlorinated tap water sold at R1/litre in South Africa, N$1/litre in Namibia. This water is available from huge clear plastic cylinders with a tap on the bottom. You bring in your own receptacle, fill it up at the tap, take it to the cashier. Simple as that. But it's not.

At one point I carried in my Land Rover two 18 litre water containers made by Coleman. These held enough water to keep me alive for around a week in the field. I only ever filled them twice from supermarket outlets, once in a Pick'n Pay in South Africa, and once in Swakopmund Spar in Namibia. Both times I enjoyed similar problems.

So, I've filled my two 18 litre containers and loaded my trolly with supplies. I go to the checkout, offload to the cashier, my bags filled by another assistant and placed in a second trolly. Finally, I heft out the water containers and tell the cashier I have two containers of 18 litres each. Confusion ensues.

I'm aware basic mathematics is not a strong point, the education system in Africa often fails to provide what it's meant to provide. I offer that the two containers total 36 litres. There is still confusion, the checkout girl chatting with animated concern to the girl packing my supplies into plastic carrier bags.

After a moment I suspect they think I'm trying to underpay. Most water containers the size of my own are 20 litre capacity. If they are familiar with this they could think I was trying to underpay by 4 litres. It does happen. It's a funny place.

After another moment I calm them down, tell the checkout girl to charge me for 40 litres. This only serves to confuse even more.

Soon both of them are behind the till looking at the screen face. I can't see bugger all from where I stand but I do note the increasing frustrations of the queue waiting behind me. Several times I ask what the problem is but am only rewarded with blank faces.

A button is pressed, a light comes on above the till. A minute or so later a supervisor appears. Animated conversation in a language I don't understand takes place along with a lot of pointing at the screen face of the till.

The supervisor asks me how much water I have. I reply two containers each of 18 litres, a total of 36 litres ... adding that if there is doubt about this then I'm more than happy to pay for 40 litres. Let's resolve this problem.

More confusion, animated voices, pointing at the screen continues.

I'm still smiling, waiting. The queue behind me is waiting but not smiling. I have no idea what the problem is but after further argument between the supervisor and checkout girl I decide 'bugger it' and walk around until I too am behind the till and can see the screen which appears to be the root cause of the problem.

To me and you it's straightforward. When someone turns up with water you touch the symbol for a bottle of water with a tap above it. The screen switches to a series of options, each in its own small square.

1L. 2L. 5L. 10L. There is also a + and a - symbol. There is a 'TOTAL' symbol. There is not an option for 36 litres. Therein lies the problem.

Taking paper and pen from the checkout counter I write down 36L. Both girls still look confused. I then ask permission to operate the touch screen. I'm allowed to. As they watch, intrigued, I touch the 10L + 10L + 10L + 5L + 1L then 'TOTAL'. Hey presto. 36L appears on the screen.

They look at me in awe. I suspect had they the power they'd nominate me for a Nobel prize.

The second time this happened I was prepared for it and the problem could have been quickly resolved. Same two containers, same confusion. I asked to come behind the till. Being me and being pretty stupid I opted to explain to this checkout girl what was required rather than doing the job myself. People have feelings and pride. I don't like stepping on them.

She caught on fast, face lighting up with understanding, almost slapping my hand away when I went to touch the first screen symbol. She wanted to do it herself. I stood back, delighted. She pressed the 1L symbol again and again and again, counting aloud all the while.

She went to 38L total and when I pointed out her mistake she all but scolded me and ushered me back to where I belonged on the other side of the counter. I went.

I paid my bill, took my supplies out to the Land Rover, packed them away in the back. Then I checked my receipt. Opposite 'Water/Drinking' was 38L - 4L. TOTAL 34L. NA$ 34.00

You can't win, can you.

****

Outlook varies as well, we don't all think the same way. Accept this as part of the country you're visiting, another interesting variation from home. That's what you came here for, isn't it? For things different from home?

O.R. Tambo airport, Johannesburg, about six months before South Africa hosted the world cup football. A fortune had been spent on the place, transforming it for the better. Keeping up appearances.

I had taken a domestic flight up from the Eastern Cape and now had a six-hour wait before my flight out to Australia. I couldn't check my bag in until three hours before departure. I opted to get something to eat and chose one of the fancy new cafes lining the concourse where I took a table.

Almost immediately a very sparky looking young girl appeared, bubbling with enthusiasm, glowing with excitement, clutching a menu.

I felt both amazed and delighted. Her smile was genuine, her enjoyment tangible. I beamed back at her. I decided she was fresh on the job, looking smart and clean and crisp in her immaculate uniform. She may only recently have finished training and felt she was now going somewhere in life, on the up. Only last week she may have been carrying water from the well on her head and living in an earth floored hut. Now she was a waitress in the big city. The world was her oyster. Those were the thoughts–be they right or wrong–that passed in a flash through my mind as I accepted the menu from her.

I found her enthusiasm and joy infectious and when she didn't move away but stood expectantly awaiting my order I didn't want to deflate her by asking her to come back in five minutes when I'd decided what to eat. Instead, I read and came to a quick decision. I wasn't too hungry, more killing time.

I looked up and she beamed down at me.

"I'll have the all-day breakfast, please. The omelette–plain please–with brown toast and coffee with milk."

I would have gone for the healthy option, coffee with doughnuts, which I'm a sucker for, but I'd noted that it was mid-day and breakfast stopped at 10AM.

Her face fell, eyes saddened.

"Breakfast is finished Sah," she stated, apology clear on her face and in her voice. She felt she was letting me down, disappointing a client when it wasn't her fault. I hate it when people call me 'sir' or 'Sah' or even worse 'baas'. The worst of the lot is being called 'comrade'. Jeez! Hasn't the world moved on? It appears not so.

"But it's an *all-day breakfast*' I pointed out, "not listed on the breakfast section but on the 'Main' section. Doesn't that mean it's available all day?" I turned the menu up to face her, finger aimed at the item of concern. She looked confused and my heart went out for her. Here she was, new to the job and trying to do her best, and she ends up with an awkward dick-head like me.

"But breakfast is finished Sah. It finished at 10AM."

"Yes, but this is an *'All Day Breakfast'*. Does that not mean it's available *'all day'*?"

She thought for a moment, then her face lit up. She took the menu from me. She'd come to a decision. She would resolve this problem.

"I will go and ask the chef for you."

She was, in her mind, doing me a favour, making allowances for me.

A minute later she returned, beaming ear to ear. She'd sorted the problem. The first day on the job, awkward and stupid customer, and she'd managed to keep the peace, give him what he wanted. What was it they said during training? Ah yes, that's it. The customer is always right.

"The chef says it's all right for you to have breakfast Sah, he will cook you what you want." She glowed with achievement and I beamed back at her.

"Ok. Thank you!"

She felt proud of her abilities even though the whole thing was a farce. Inside I applauded her.

"I'll have a plain omelette with brown toast, coffee with milk please."

(I find it ridiculous that we now have to tip-toe through life, ordering coffee with or without milk, for fear of offending delicate sensibilities. Do people faint with shock when they look at themselves in the mirror? What do they see reflected? And who, in all honesty, are we offending? If we persist in making colour an issue then it will remain an issue.)

She smiled with genuine pleasure, then a slow shadow fell over her face.

"And filling Sah? What fillings do you want?"

Oh dear. I smiled and informed her I wanted a plain omelette, no fillings.

"But the omelette comes with 3 fillings" she pointed out, forgiving me for my stupidity and feeling a little embarrassed by having to bring this to notice. It was obvious I was a bit simple. I detected a touch of sympathy in her quiet speech.

I stared at her for a moment, a blank look on my face, this only confirming I was simple. Sometimes I forget I'm in Africa.

She leant forwards, her smile returning though a little strained now. Her long (without milk) finger tapped on the menu in my hands, indicating the selection of fillings available. I'll admit 'plain' was not listed. Cheese, mushroom, ham, spring onion, chilli, capsicum, tomato, and spinach were. I could choose up to three fillings all included in the price. Therein lay the problem.

I put on what I hoped was my most winning, understanding smile.

"Yes, I know, thank you, but all I want is a plain omelette, no filling thanks. I'm not a big eater, not too hungry. A plain omelette, no filling, will be fine."

Here I was, trying to be gentle and polite with this well-meaning soul, all but apologising for my choice of food.

She looked aghast and I knew I was onto a looser. No way was I going to get away with a plain omelette when–for the same money–I could have one with **THREE** fillings. Why in hell should I want to pay good money and receive half the potential?

I knew what I wanted and was happy paying the price. It was what I desired.

She could not comprehend this. To her it was lunacy. It was obvious I was missing something, not all there. Not only that but I suspect there was a touch of personal, even professional pride in all this. She wanted me to get the best deal for my money, couldn't make the jump and understand why I would wish otherwise. She was fulfilling what she saw as her obligation to the client. To get them the best deal, to make them happy. How could anyone be happy paying good money for an omelette without filling when they could have three fillings included in the price. It didn't make sense. She was looking after me. I probably looked a bit skinny to her anyway. Maybe her mothering instincts came into play even though she was less than half my age.

A bit of too and fro began, me trying to convince her all I wanted was a plain omelette, she doing her best to politely persuade me of my stupidity.

I ordered an omelette with chilli, ham and cheese. She left happy, victorious even.

It was a nice omelette. She was a delightful and sincere waitress. I left a good tip. I got breakfast–the all day one–and a story.

****

And then there is the other side of the coin, the side where it's me that's left feeling stupid.

My sis had accompanied me on a road trip up from South Africa. We'd entered Namibia via the Kgalagadi Trans-frontier Park then spent a week in Damaraland. I was remaining in Namibia for a few months while my sis flew back to South Africa. The night before her flight was due we stopped at a small lodge and campsite within easy driving distance from the airport. Her phone wasn't working in Namibia and I hadn't bothered getting a new SIM card for my own. My sis wanted to call her husband to confirm her flight the following day so I bought a SIM card which I'd be able to use during the coming months.

I'm a bit shambolic about these things and owning the latest technology has never been of interest. My phone at the time was an ancient flip phone, it's only functions texts and calls. When I fitted the new SIM I threw the packaging away without taking a note of the number. Not very bright, I know.

In the bar that night I asked the girl serving us if I could send her a text and in that way find out the number of my new SIM. She took my phone, rolled her eyes at its simplicity and antiquity, sent a text to her smart phone, and then informed me of my new number. When she handed my phone back I teased her by asking her if I now had her number. She looked at me as though I were some kind of simpleton jerk, not too far from the truth.

"No," she smiled, "I erased it."

Sensible girl.

A couple of weeks later I was back in the area, this time for a meeting in Windhoek. I took a room in the same lodge and then spent some time on Google Maps trying to find the location for the following days meeting. No joy, the street names had changed, a common practise in countries where independence has been gained. Think dogs pissing on posts.

I went to the bar, bought a beer. It was the same barmaid who'd helped me get my new phone number and she remembered me. We chatted for a bit, the only other customers sitting on bar stools, eyes focused on screens, playing with their smart phones in the way people do these days. I told her of my problem and asked her if she knew where the offices were, explaining the address I had was 'corner of' two streets that didn't appear on Google maps.

She wasn't sure and after a moment involved the three others at the bar in our conversation, explaining my problem, giving the address and asking them if they knew where the building was. None of them could be sure either.

"Why don't you use your phone?" suggested the guy at the end of the bar, holding his own piece of smart technology up as a reference.

"Eeeehh!" breathed the barmaid, eyes wide with amused astonishment. "Have you seen his phone!"

The Parable of the Jacket

It was June, the middle of a Namibian winter, the coldest month of the year. Many people assume that because much of Namibia is desert it must always be hot. That's not so. Deserts can suffer extremes in temperature, from blistering hot during the day to freezing at night. The deserts of Namibia are no different and those areas lying close to the Atlantic coast are further affected by the cold Benguela current flowing north from the Antarctic.

Much of desert temperature variation is due to elevation and cloud cover. Clear, cloudless skies offer no protection from the sun during the day. Come nightfall those same clear skies offer no layer of insulation retaining the day's built-up heat. Imagine good cloud cover as a down quilt.

Winter in the arid areas of Namibia usually consists of near-freezing nights and long, slow warm-ups from cold mornings. Come lunchtime you're usually discarding clothes like a stripper on speed.

Many visitors fail to grasp this information even though it's mentioned on websites and brochures and most safari companies offer seasonal packing lists according to location. Not everyone reads these things and the group myself and another guide were looking after on this trip had a couple of such people.

It was a four-day/three-night trip, the aim being to find and view desert-adapted elephants while spotting other game along the way. We already knew the elephants were well downriver from us, a very long and demanding drive away. This would be hard on the car, fuel and driver, and uncomfortable, dusty and gruelling for the clients. We hoped the elephants might turn around and head back upriver, meeting us halfway.

The first night out we camped well away from the river, high among the drainage valleys and koppies of the south bank. The dry river bed and its wide swathes of riparian vegetation are like a linear oasis, a wide green serpent weaving between the sun-blasted hills of red rock and sand on its way to the distant ocean. In thtime-eroded gorges and canyons the dry river constricts and narrows, trees and scrub making use of every patch of flat, deep soil before the often vertical cliffs deny them purchase for roots or access to underground water. In the wider, flatter areas the vegetation spreads out like spilt oil, utilising every inch of ground that can support it. Not only is this weaving and twisting dry water course a linear oasis it is also a highway for wildlife. It's a thoroughfare offering food and water, shade and shelter, and cover for both prey and predator. For these reasons, it's not a good idea to set up camp in a dry riverbed. There is also the risk of flash floods though this is seasonal. But for many it's the preferred place, offering shade, soft sand and firewood. I often compare camping in a river bed to pitching your tent on a motorway. If you don't get hit by passing traffic you're going to disrupt it. Setting up camp well back from the river bed allows all other life to flow along unimpeded and reduces the risk of human/ wildlife conflict. It's safer. I also believe that in winter it's warmer to camp above river beds rather than in them. Cold air is denser and sinks to the lowest point.

Regardless of the fact we camped well back from the river our camp was a cold one with temperatures dropping as darkness fell. It always feels coldest in the hours immediately each side of dawn and the following morning was no different. As everyone huddled around last night's rejuvenated fire, sipping from enamel mugs of steaming tea or coffee and savouring the heat seeping through to their fingers, I noticed two of our guests didn't have warm jackets. Others had taken the advice offered before departure and wore heavy jackets or fleeces, woollen beanies, jeans, thick socks and boots. Some also wore light gloves. But as usual there were a couple who either hadn't bothered reading the suggested packing list or assumed because it was Africa it was going to be hot. These two were dressed in shorts and cotton shirts, heads and legs left bare. Like everyone else, their breath steamed as they squatted close to the fire. Any closer and they would have been in it. Their teeth chattered and they shivered in the frigid early morning air. They might be suffering now but things would get worse before the sun began to make itself felt around mid-morning. In half an hour they would be sitting on the raised and exposed seats of an open game-viewing vehicle and they'd have the additional pleasures of wind-chill to deal with.

I was never cut out for guiding, never planned to be a guide, it's something I fell into and most of what's entailed I enjoy. I love being out in the bush, the smaller the group the better. I love the unplanned freedom of wild camping and cooking over open fires. I love the star-studded night skies, sharp and crisp and clear of light pollution–especially when viewed from a warm sleeping bag. I enjoy the challenge of off-road driving. Even more, I enjoy trail walking through the ancient crumpled and battered topography of Damaraland, journeying by foot allowing access to places most others never visit. Most of all I love the wildlife and imparting what little knowledge I have about it to interested guests. With the right people, the sharing of information and understanding can be more rewarding than receiving it. It can be a bit like giving gifts to loved ones at Christmas, or anytime for that matter. What I don't like about guiding is that on many occasions the 'right people' seem few and far between. Good guides own many skills and dealing with a wide spectrum of guests, being a 'people's person,' is the most important one. For that reason alone I would never term myself a good guide.

I looked at our two guests shivering and shuddering as they crouched close to the dying fire. They were cold, uncomfortable, unhappy and probably wondering what they were doing here and wishing they'd never come. Their discomfort was of their own doing but if I were to do my job–hell, be a decent person–it was up to me to do something about it. Putting my coffee aside I dug in our stores and found a couple of extra blankets we carried for such situations. I gave one of these to each of the suffering guests who draped themselves in the warm coverings.

I was wearing a thigh-length green shooting jacket over a T-shirt and light fleece. It was a good jacket, a very expensive jacket designed to withstand the rigours of a Scottish winter. I'd had it for years, treasured it, and found it well suited for frigid desert mornings. I took it off and offered it to them, explaining that I would spend the day driving and though the Land Cruiser's cab was open I'd have more protection from wind chill than they would sitting above the cargo bed. One guest hesitated, a touch too polite. The other grabbed it, no scruples.

Half an hour later we were all packed up and ready to go. Once everyone was seated I stood alongside the vehicle and gave a short briefing about our planned route and what the day might entail. I noticed the lady who had accepted my jacket with such alacrity had positioned herself in the well-protected centre seat in a row of three, sheltered on each side by another's body. My heavy jacket was zipped up tight, high collar raised against the breeze. Her lap and legs were wrapped in the blanket. She'd be warm enough.

The morning wasn't encouraging, a long drive downriver. Now and then we'd stop and I'd explain fresh tracks left in the river sand. The elephant family group we were following remained elusive. They were on a mission, a day ahead of us and moving downriver fast and with purpose rather than sauntering along and browsing at will as they do when relaxed.

Throughout the length of the dry riverbed, there are springs where the underground water is forced to the surface by impervious bands of rock. These springs vary in size depending on the obstruction and how far it extends. At lunchtime, we arrived at the last of these springs in that section of the river. If the elephants hadn't stopped here then the next water was almost a full day's drive further downriver, a gruelling trip for vehicles and passengers. The spring covers a very large area, the central part being a wide sea of tall reeds walled in by towering shale cliffs. So tall and dense is this huge reed bed it can conceal even elephants. We parked close to the base of an angled cliff and those enthusiastic enough accompanied me high above the vehicle. The elevation would offer a much better chance of spotting the great, grey backs of the elephants if they were feeding among the reeds. They weren't. For half an hour we sat in the now warm sunshine and scanned the sea of green stretching far downriver, searching with binoculars for grey backs peeping above the vegetation, or the sway and movement of tall reeds as something large pushed through them. Finally, we accepted the animals were not there and must have moved on downriver with little more than a halt to drink. We clambered back down to the vehicle and joined the others for lunch. I noticed the lady who had borrowed my jacket had discarded it and was sitting enjoying the sun in her shirt sleeves. I didn't comment, didn't think it was necessary.

Though we were now in a remote and seldom visited area we did see one other vehicle soon after lunch. It was a game drive vehicle from a local lodge, like us out looking for elephants, a small party of guests seated in the back. We chatted with their guide and informed him of our thoughts on the group of elephants we were following. Unlike us, they were out only for the day and had limited time. They followed us at a distance down through the spring but when we failed to find elephants in the section remaining they left us, turning around and heading back to the lodge before darkness and temperatures fell.

We continued downstream a short distance until a suitable exit from the gorge-like river bed allowed us into the surrounding hills to make camp. It was a cold evening and once things were organised and dinner being prepared I went in search of my jacket. It wasn't in the back of the Land Cruiser so I found the lady I'd given it to and asked its whereabouts. She didn't know. She'd given it to the other woman suffering cold mid-morning and hadn't seen it since. I asked this second lady who informed me she'd worn it till lunchtime and that it must still be in the vehicle. I told her it wasn't so we both went to take a look. No joy. It had disappeared. I could only guess it had been put aside and then fallen off the truck later on. This in itself was frustrating and annoying. More disappointing was the fact that neither of the two women responsible seemed in the least bit concerned. If roles had been reversed I would have been mortified by the loss, apologised, accepted responsibility and insisted on replacing the item with something similar as soon as possible. But there was no apology, not a hint of consideration, concern or regret. Just a shrug of the shoulders and a disinterested return to the warmth of the fire. From what I've read even Queen Elizabeth acknowledged Sir Walter Raleigh's chivalry when he laid his cloak over a puddle she had to cross.

There are guests, even groups of guests, I'm more than happy to see the back of, and I'm sure there have been many guests happy to see the back of me. There are times, at the end of a trip you part company with guests feeling a tinge of regret. They were nice people, easy-going, considerate and friendly. You worked hard and hope they have fond memories not just of you but of all they've seen and experienced. On this trip, I had reservations about some of the group from the outset. The complete indifference shown by the loss of my jacket confirmed initial misgivings.

The following morning we began to retrace the previous afternoon's route in the hope of picking the jacket up along the way but to no avail. No sign of the jacket and time spent looking for it ate into guest time with elephants or viewing other game. After only half an hour we turned around and continued our way downriver.

We did find elephants and the viewing was excellent. We parked up and the small herd came to us, browsing without concern close around the vehicle for over two hours. We also enjoyed good sightings of giraffe, gemsbok and springbok before time forced us to leave the area and return to camp via dirt tracks offering a shorter and smoother trip which lacked the diversity and excitement of the river route.

The final night was the usual group dinner back in town and for a while I considered not attending. It hadn't been the best of trips, relationships between myself and some of the guests deteriorating as the days passed. I knew I wasn't flavour of the month and as far as I was concerned it was unlikely I'd shed any tears if I were never to see some of that group again. In the end, I decided it would be churlish not to attend, and besides, not everyone in the group considered me pond life.

It was a large group and cliques had formed. More by chance than management I ended up sitting close to the end of the long table, those around me not too hostile. The atmosphere remained pleasant, the conversation lively with me doing the best I could to entertain and satisfy curiosities.

Towards the end of the evening, one of those present asked why HIV remained so prevalent in much of Africa while in other countries it was in decline. A valid question, but not one I particularly wanted to answer. It's a touchy subject. The continuing HIV problem stems from many different causes. Some are cultural, some due to stigma, some from belief, and some from social behaviour. I'd been down this, and similar roads, before. It never matters how you construct your phrases or how well you put things, in some people's opinions you end up being a critical, racist bastard. Conforming to political correctness often involves veiling the facts, the truth. From experience, I knew that stating things as they are can lead to heated exchanges, usually because what's stated doesn't conform to what others perceive they should believe. Sometimes it's as though holding views and thoughts–even worse having the temerity to state them–based on undeniable facts and personal experience, is no longer acceptable. I now try to sidestep these potential minefields.

I could have been flippant and said 'the locals like to shag a lot'. But I didn't. It was a sincere question and deserved an honest explanation, the best I could offer.

I looked down the table at my two jacket-losing friends who turned their attentions back to one another and resumed chatting. Hmmm???

"Remember that nice jacket I lost this past week?" I began, and several of the listening group nodded, though a touch confused by what my lost jacket had to do with HIV problems in Africa.

"It was last seen around lunchtime, about the same time as we first saw the other safari vehicle from the lodge." Again there were nods of agreement.

"The following morning we retraced some of our previous days's route in the hope of picking the jacket up, but to no avail, there was no sign of it."

More nods of agreement and more looks of confusion. Where was this going? I wasn't too sure myself.

"It's possible the lodge vehicle picked up my jacket, the guide putting it out of sight and assuring his guests he'd hand it in to reception on their return."

Most of the table was listening by this time. We all love a good story. I continued.

"This guide has social standing in the community. He's educated, qualified, drives a lodge vehicle and wears the lodge apparel. He mixes with wealthy overseas visitors and even eats dinner with some of them. He has kudos and doesn't want to lose it. Hanging onto a jacket he picked up from the track could stigmatise him."

The whole table was listening now though I won't say all with happy faces.

"That night he buys a couple of big bottles of beer and goes to visit a woman who recently moved into the area. She's from up North, has a young son, and no husband present. Like most, she's come to the area in the hope of getting work at the lodge. She's happy to do anything. But work is scarce, there are many vying for the same jobs, and there is a local hierarchy of first come, first served. She's well down the queue. In the interim, to make ends meet, she's decided to get some goats. The communal grazing is free. Goats will provide milk, meat, skin, and a source of income. But how to pay for them, get onto that first rung of the ladder? The evening goes well. The guide leaves without the jacket."

"A couple of days later this same woman, wearing the nice, warm jacket, visits one of the wealthier farmers in the area. He has four wives, fifteen children, a good pick-up truck and income enough to support several less fortunate members of his extended family. They agree the jacket is worth one young goat. He selects a young female from his flock, a pregnant female which might yet produce twins. But of course, now he'd need more than the jacket in payment."

"This farmer's youngest wife is a bit of an old man's folly, a vanity. He's been ignoring her of late, knows she's unhappy and worries she may be cuckolding him. He brings her the jacket and she's all over him like a rash. The gift has elevated her. She may be the most junior wife but the jacket shows consideration, even favouritism. She caters to his every whim in appreciation."

"But the old farmer is right about being cuckolded. It was an arranged marriage. Her lover since schooldays had little chance of raising a bridal price. She still sees him regularly. He looks after another man's goats in the hills upriver. The next time she visits she takes him the jacket. It will keep him warm on those freezing winter mornings when the wind cuts through clothing like a knife."

"He's from poor stock with no real prospects. The last twenty years have been shit and the next twenty don't look any brighter. He finds solace in alcohol and with empty pockets he visits a local shebeen, trading the jacket for beer. The woman who owns the shebeen is a hard nut and drives a hard bargain but even she has to accept the jacket is worth more than a few bottles of beer. There is no way she is handing out cash for it but she doesn't want to lose his trade. An alternative solution is found, one that costs her nothing but a little of her time."

"A couple of days later her generator breaks down. It's due out on hire at a funeral and she's desperate. There is only one guy living locally who's capable of fixing it, and he's well aware of this. She hates parting with money unless she's sure she can get it back over the counter. The guy who can fix her generator doesn't drink. She offers the jacket but it's not enough. How much would it cost her to call someone out from town to get the generator fixed? How long would she have to wait before it happened? He's right of course. He's got her over a barrel, literally and figuratively."

"It's now early Monday morning, two weeks since my jacket was lost. I'm sitting in camp, enjoying coffee and a smoke before the day's work begins. I'm about eighty kilometres from where the jacket disappeared. The local guys start appearing, walking in from the settlement at the bridge. One of them is wearing my jacket."

A Bit of a Rant

I'm writing this essay from a small camp high above the dry Ugab River in Damaraland, Namibia. It's Christmas 2021 and the effects of COVID are still felt worldwide.

I've spent the past three months in Botswana, living in a basic but adequate cabin on the lush banks of the Thamalakane River with crocs and hippos and fish eagles for neighbours. I'm now back in bare rock and mountainous desert. The contrasts are staggering. From dense riparian forest and flat Kalahari bush to the tumbled boulder and sun-blasted mountains of Damaraland. Here brown and orange are the predominant colours, and plants and animals are few and far between. Being one thousand kilometres further west the sun rises and sets later than what I've become familiar with. The light, especially in late afternoon, has a sharpness, an intensity so harsh it hurts the eyes.

Botswana was entering its rainy season with oppressive heat and high humidity. Thunder clouds built over several days before finally releasing their contents in torrential downpours which battered off the tin roof of my shack like a thousand drummers gone crazy. The frequent light shows and drum rolls from night-time thunder and lightning storms were a soul-lifting display of elemental power. Sand-tracks filled with pools of deep water making them all but impassable.

Here in Namibia, the rains have yet to appear. Nights and mornings are cool. Around lunchtime the north-west wind arrives. Afternoons are like standing before a fan oven with the door wide open, the dragon's breath breeze drying sweat before it can form. Dust trails follow every vehicle.

I know where I'm happiest. It's here in the desert. I can never be sure why this is. It may be because of the horizons, the sense of space and timelessness the desert offers, and its ability to make you feel inconsequential. The desert, like mountains, like oceans, doesn't care. But the desert has a paucity that includes its concern.

The camp I'm in belongs to a large safari company that uses it as a staging post during their mobile safaris. There are nine luxury tents complete with ensuite bathrooms with flushing toilets and showers. Placed downslope from the tents and overlooking the Ugab River there is a central, open-sided, thatched roof 'boma', generally used as a communal meeting and eating area. I have access to a fridge, a gas stove and slow internet. There is no phone service. It's the kind of place I rant and rave against and I never thought I'd end up staying here. The combination of COVID and the owner's generosity has allowed differently.

Four years ago, on invitation, I came to this very camp to give a lecture on desert-adapted elephants. The client group was from the UK, enthusiastic naturalists. At that time the owner company was greenwashing, making declarations of eco-consciousness that were downright lies. Like so many other morally bankrupt safari companies they were in for the quick profit rather than the long-term benefit.

After I'd given the usual lecture on desert-adapted elephants the audience wanted to know what environmental and ecological problems the area suffered. I did hesitate, wondered how open and honest I should be with these high-paying, well-meaning people who'd travelled a long way to gain experience of southwest Africa. Then I thought 'fuck it'. In a long-winded way I told them it was safari companies and camps like the one they were patronising that were much of the problem. That they as visitors were contributing. That over-use of precious resources like water and mopani woodlands would have long-term effects. Even the elephants themselves were being over-exploited and within my limited experience I believed now showed signs of stress.

Twice the camp manager and guide tried to shut me up. Give them their due, the audience wanted to know more, wanted the truth, even from an outspoken bastard like myself. I often wonder if they took anything away with them or if it was all forgotten by the next morning, not even a distant memory the next time they went to book a safari.

To be fair and give credit where credit is due, the camp has cleaned its act up. The diesel-powered generator has gone, replaced by a bank of solar panels. The wood-burning donkey boilers, used to heat each individual tent's water, are gone, solar water heaters now doing the job. The open fire pit in the braai area, there for safari ambience more than heat, is now small. The fuel used is briquettes of alien species rather than the native mopane once touted as the same. They still have flushing toilets–in a desert.

For years I've been a strong critic of the way the safari industry is going here, condemning the needless waste of water in particular. But it's a self-feeding circle. Tourists have come to expect, even demand a certain standard, and if one safari company offers all the comforts of a five-star hotel then so must all the others. Those self-entitled, unthinking tourists need education. The safari industry needs regulation and monitoring.

To my way of thinking it's simple. If you're going to visit a desert, don't expect a lot of water. There isn't any. That's why it's called a desert. Buckle down, accept where you are and the restrictions location place upon you. Stop whining about comforts. It's a trade-off. You 'suffer' a minor lack of 'comforts'. You gain by experiencing a wonderful place and do so with limited impact.

Africa is not Europe or North America or anywhere else. It's Africa and that's why you go to see it. Things are very different, this being part of the adventure, the attraction. So why take your excessive Western expectations with you? Should it not be a case of 'when in Rome'?

I've seen locals when first shown a flushing toilet, look in horrified amazement and I know what's going through their heads–'What, you shit in the water in your country?' In much of Africa, water is gold. Southern Africa is water-poor. Very few rural homes have piped water, the daily requirements are carried from communal taps or wells in whatever container is available. It's not unusual to see women with 20-litre water carriers on their heads. They use it sparingly and not only because it has to be carried from source to home, but because it's a valued resource in limited supply. Through necessity, they've learned to be frugal, to use it with respect.

Then we turn up, as high-paying tourists, and insist on two showers each day, a good long hair wash to clean out that terrible dust from the game drives on open vehicles, and flushing toilets.

Once more, we as Westerners, are exploiting and diminishing vital resources just as we did with the wildlife and much of the land. Haven't we learned anything?

In addition to this much of southern Africa suffers the same problem as the rest of the world, a burgeoning population. Here in Namibia, the government is attempting to prevent migration from rural areas to the city and all the associated problems this brings. Rural dwellers are offered incentives to remain in the country and farm. In much of the country, poor soil conditions and a lack of rainfall dictate livestock farming, crops are not an option. But livestock needs water and to this end more and more boreholes are drilled and artificial water points established.

So who's at fault? All of us are; rural dwellers with their livestock, commercial farmers with theirs, us tourists and the safari companies who cater to us. But we, the tourists and safari companies, can do something about it. We don't have to use the amount of water we currently demand.

The safari industry is a competitive business with many companies fishing from the same pond. To attract high-paying clientele companies up their game, offering greater comfort, five-star accommodation, high-level cuisine, enclosed game drive vehicles with air conditioning, a cooler full of iced drinks, and bespoke itineraries. The days of basic canvas tents, oil lamps and bucket showers a la 'Out of Africa' are almost long gone–though still available if you're into retro and fancy yourself as a bit of a Robert Redford or Meryl Streep.

And we as tourists have come to expect all these luxuries. We don't want to step out of that comfort bubble. There has to be cell service, internet, ad-lib hot water, flushing toilets, comfortable dust-free vehicles with air-con, the best food and copious amounts of wine. It's an artificial environment, it's not Africa. It's Western expectations transported to Africa. What's that all about?

Why not settle in front of the TV at home with all its comforts and amenities and watch natural history documentaries, save yourself some discomfort and money?

That's not to say all safari companies and all tourists are the same. Many from both sides of the coin endeavour to minimise impact, keep things simple and basic and leave a smaller footprint. That's the way it has to go. Like everything else on this planet, Africa is a limited resource and if we're not careful we're going to love the place to death.

I've worked with camps that offer only bucket showers, restricting each client to ten litres of washing water each day. Toilets have been long drop or compost affairs. Laundry service is unavailable until you return to town or opt to wash items in the shower while you use it. And why not? And these are safari companies that charge like a wounded buffalo. And still people come. I'm convinced, among many, there is a growing desire to do something different, to step out of the comfort bubble and to leave a smaller footprint.

There are several examples substantiating this belief. The one that springs first to mind is a mountain camp located not too far from where I sit. It was a low-key but expensive camp where walking the arid mountains was the only offered activity. No vehicle game drives were available. I applauded that. I also applauded the fact that high-paying clients could use only twenty litres of water per day. They could use this as they desired but that was it. Twenty litres, no more. Contrary to what you'd imagine the place did well. In fact, it did so well that one of the larger safari groups which tend to absorb anything they consider competition, or that might turn a profit, took it over a couple of years back. The camp now sports a swimming pool. It's halfway up an arid mountain, in a desert. Clients are no longer water rationed.

The long-term effects of our current behaviours and attitudes could be serious. The rivers here are dry for ten months of the year and when they do flow it's seldom for more than two or three days. Boreholes now proliferate, following the paths of these ephemeral systems, lowering the water table. And it is happening. Many boreholes sunk only ten years ago are already defunct. Others have been bored again, sinking deeper to reach the diminishing underground reserves. Soon it's possible the tap roots of riparian trees will no longer be able to reach the water. The trees will die. Shade, food, and shelter will disappear. The root systems holding fragile topsoil together will vanish and wind and flood will sweep it away. When the food source goes so will the animals. Desertification, hastened along by the expectations of self-indulgent tourists who appear incapable of existing without flushing toilets and two showers each day. Even worse are those lodges touting wet rooms and an oh-so-necessary plunge pool where you can float chin-deep while viewing the wildlife and sipping your G&T.

'Oh darling, I'd absolutely die if I couldn't wash my hair every night before dinner. Just what would I look like!' (uttered to me, eyes wide with shock-horror, in a camp in Botswana)

I have to ask, after a statement like that, what do you look like.

For sure there is always initial doubt and uncertainty when people first step out from their familiar comfort bubble. We need time to adapt. But once the leap is made, when people realise they are not going to die because they can't wash their hair for half an hour or luxuriate for long minutes beneath high-pressure jets of hot water, then it all becomes a bit of an adventure, a new challenge in ways. What's more these same people tend to feel better about themselves. They are not leaving a large footprint, not damaging the balance of things by their presence. I also believe they begin to 'feel' the place more; the dust on their skin, up their noses, in their hair, powdering their clothing; the salt of dried sweat on their cheeks and lips; the softness and familiarity of much worn clothing rather than the clinical crispness of clean garments; the camaraderie of all being in this together and realising it doesn't matter if you get sweaty and dusty during the day, sweaty and dusty is the bush in Africa, part and parcel of it all. Finally, there is the value placed on that one brief shower. It becomes a precious and much-appreciated occasion, something to look forward to. Water is prized. It's savoured and no longer taken for granted. If people can take that home with them, no matter where they live, that has to be a good thing.

I've been returning here for more than a decade now. Even in that short period I've noted the changes. None of them have been for the long term better.

A project I've been involved with, on-and-off, concerns human/animal conflict. Elephants are the main 'problem' animals and the conflicts are over resources, primarily water.

When I was involved the project relied on paying volunteers. Like so many safari companies and wildlife projects it worried that should clients feel they are going to suffer too much 'hardship' they may not sign on. I don't believe that to be true. For sure you may lose some clients but you wouldn't lose them all. And those you do lose... well, you're probably better off without them.

At times I've attempted to persuade some of these paying volunteers over to my way of thinking. I'd be delighted when I met those who didn't need persuasion, heartened by those, especially the younger generations, who thought big-picture and understood.

I tried to do this gently, talking to people over dinner. I'd ask why each of them had chosen to volunteer. I was also interested in what makes others spend time and money on a project such as this.

Why, to help rare desert-adapted elephants of course, would be the reply.

What's the problem with elephants? I'd ask.

They are in conflict with humans.

Why conflict?

Over resources, we are in competition with them, encroaching on their habitat.

And what's the main resource we are in conflict with elephants over? What have you come here to do?

We are here to protect water points and stop the elephants from destroying them while offering them alternative drinking options.

Right, so the real conflict is water?

Yes.

Ok, it's a desert. All resources, including water, are in short supply. The water table is dropping. Elephants now struggle to dig deep enough to reach underground sources as they once did. They also now have available artificial, man-made, water points. Why bother digging for fresh water when it's there, right in front of you in bloody great tanks. In some cases, they have little alternative. Damage often occurs, elephants not having a huge understanding of plumbing systems. The best way any of you can assist elephants is by not using 'their' water, ensuring there is enough remaining for the future. Go easy on the showering, the washing up, the tooth brushing, the hair washing. You'll be back in civilisation before you know it. Contribute by not taking too much away.

I'd often get total silence to that one, as though they all sat there thinking 'What, I have to inconvenience myself?'

I suspect some of them only came on the project to increase their popularity on Facebook.

I'd mention the use of camp showers, detailing how to take an 'army' shower. You run water only long enough to get wet then switch off. You lather up, all over, and when soaped you rinse off, using only the necessary amount of water.

That often fell on deaf ears as well.

I tried highlighting the fact that taking a shower immediately before heading into the bush for a week was pointless. Within the hour they would be dust and sweat-covered and that's how they would remain all week.

Very few takers.

I asked why some insisted on a long hot shower before boarding the minibus for the four-hour drive back to Swakopmund. Once there they could take an even hotter and longer shower–and probably would anyway–courtesy of the town's desalinated water supply. They were all dusty and smelly. Why not tough it out for one more morning? What did it matter?

The showers were often busy right up until the mini bus was ready to go.

While preparing vehicles in the workshop area, making them ready to go out for several days of patrol in the bush, I'd often see a queue forming for the showers. At times I'd hear people complain someone else was taking too long, especially when they'd already been in there twenty minutes. I'd want to stamp my feet, wave my arms, scream and shout, throw a good tantrum, well and truly spit the dummy.

You took a shower last night you selfish morons. You're going into the field for four days. You won't have water to wash. You are going to be sweaty and dusty within the first hour and it's not going to get any better until you return. Do you think the elephants will care? Who are you doing this for? Yourself? To make you 'feel' better? Or are you doing it because you worry about what others might think of you? For god's sake get a grip. You're in a bloody desert!

What is it with us? Why can't we go a whole week without taking a shower? Are we going to fade away and die if we don't get clean? Yes, I know it's nice to feel washed and fresh, but this is a desert and water is scarce. It's only sweat and grime on your body, not sulphuric acid. If you had to get down on your hands and knees on the river bed's sandy floor and dig with bare fingers for water to wash in, would you do it? Would you make the effort of digging two, maybe three metres down before the bottom of the hole began to fill? No, of course you wouldn't. You'd go smelly for the week rather than put all that effort in.

My solution to the problem ... take the water away, then no one can abuse it.

Get a grip. Bloody tourists.

Okay, rant over.

I'm staying in this upmarket safari camp because I'm once more trying to write. It offers the peace and quiet I appear to need for such an endeavour. And this camp, like so many others all over Africa–all over the world, due to COVID–currently sits empty. No bookings until May and even then it's a handful, and they are not guaranteed. Here it is, sitting among the rugged rock outcrops overlooking the dry sand bed of the Ugab River, and it's empty. Nine tents with en-suite, a central boma with outside braai area, an open-air kitchen, and not a soul about. There is a local caretaker and his delightful wife, here to discourage theft more than anything. If they were not here the whole camp would disappear in days. The very minimal rent I'm paying will help cover his salary, and keep him in a job.

Did I hear a gasp? Are you shocked that a safari camp might disappear in days were it not for the full-time caretaker and his wife being present? Oh please, let's be realistic. The majority of those living locally own little more than the clothing they stand up in. Of course things would disappear. There would be queues of battered old pick-up trucks, people with wheel barrows or donkey carts, all loaded to the gunnels. Those without transport would carry items balanced on their heads, all marching back down the hill before scattering to the four winds, the items removed never to be seen again. Everything would go. In less than a week it would be difficult to tell there had once been a camp here. Even the water pipes would be dug up and taken away. Oh, hang on. They would leave the flushing toilets and the showers, they have more sense than use them in a desert.

Tell me, do you have locks on your doors and windows and do you use them, and if so why? Does your car have an alarm and immobilisation system and do you utilise it? Does your insurance company insist you have these systems fitted to your car? Do you padlock your bike to a lamp post before leaving it?

People are the same the world over, no matter race or colour, creed or religion. At least here, where I am, it's understandable, even forgivable, people covet other's belongings so much.

This is my first morning here. I rose before dawn and walked in the semi-darkness from my tent down to the kitchen area alongside the central boma. I boiled water and made coffee then moved to the outside braai area which overlooks the near vertical drop down into the dry Ugab River. There is a low wall built above this drop. This low wall is wide and at the midpoint has several large cemented indents designed to hold water and attract bird life. They were empty. No tourists to entertain, no need to have birds crapping everywhere. I sat and sipped my coffee, smoked a cigarette, and watched the sun begin to rise from behind the high cliffs on the far side of the river. With the light came the birds. They began to gather and I imagined they were looking at me in expectation. 'Come on mate, where's the bleedin water?' kind of thing.

I went to the kitchen area, filled two large kettles with water and used them to fill the sealed indents on the low wall. Then I sat back to watch. It didn't take long which rather surprised me.

Many of the creatures living in desert environments are water-independent. They don't need to drink. And it's not just lizards and snakes and other reptiles that have this ability to live without water. Here in Namibia, several mammals are so well adapted they may go years without actually drinking, their moisture requirements fulfilled from early morning dew on the vegetation and from the little liquid obtained from the vegetation itself. There are physiological adaptations as well, some of them fascinating, especially in the case of gemsbok. But this is not a biology lesson, it's a rant about concerns and misplaced expectations.

So I sat there, not more than five metres from these small pools of shallow water and watched as things developed. You might be asking why are there so many birds if there is no surface water. Good question. Birds have mobility, they can fly to distant water points. But why burn energy and use scarce resources flying a round trip of ten kilometres when there is water on your doorstep?

Within minutes there had to be over fifty birds surrounding the water pools. Pale-winged starlings, fork-tailed drongos, a couple of rock pigeons, red-eyed bulbuls, babblers, rosey-faced love birds, masked weavers and an assortment of little brown jobs I couldn't identify without a reference book. Most amazing was the appearance of a pair of red billed francolin, a ground-dwelling partridge-like bird that inhabits the sparse riparian vegetation far below in the river bed. These francolins must have climbed a hundred feet up the rock-tumbled slope to reach the water. How did they know? And so soon? Did other bird calls of excitement make them aware there was water once more on offer? Did they notice other birds gathering and curiosity got the better of them? Do birds call to those of their own species saying 'there's water here' and the francolin recognise this call?

The water attracted more than birds. From among the cracked and fissured rocks appeared dassies (rock hyrax) and dassie rats (smaller mammals with long bushy tails). I sat still and watched. They were aware of my close presence but bit by bit the temptation of cool clear water overcame their natural caution. Before long they too were enjoying a gentle drink. I was, as usual, thrilled. I also felt I'd contributed, given wildlife a bit of a gift, and made their day as they were now making my own.

Then my preconceived assumptions collapsed. First one bird–a little brown job–then another, and another, entered the water and began to bathe. Within moments the pools were a teeming mass of bird life, like the shallow end of a swimming pool full of excited children, the only thing missing being the high-pitched screams of delight. Heads were ducked below the surface then lifted and shaken. Wings fluttered so the air filled with a myriad of sparkling silver droplets. Then the dassies and the dassie rats joined in, slithering into the pool like miniature beavers, squirming their bodies beneath the surface before clambering back out and shaking dry, looking oh so pleased with themselves.

Here, right before my disbelieving eyes, wildlife carelessly abused a good clear pool of water. They were squandering a resource that in this arid outback is worth more than gold, fouling it with dust and their parasite-ridden bodies. Taking a shower. Taking a bath!

Bloody wildlife.

Sod it. I'm off for a shower.

Also by Colin Valentine

Bibbulmun for the Broken-Hearted
Damaraland
African Essays

About the Author

Raised in rural Scotland Colin Valentine developed a keen interest in wild places and wild animals from a young age. These have been constants throughout his life and are now main themes in his writing. He's a firm believer that the only way to truly experience anywhere is by travelling slowly, on foot.

For the past two decades he's split most of his time between Australia where he's lived out of the back of a Subaru, and southern Africa where he lives out of a Land Rover. During these decades he's indulged his interests while attempting to give something back through commitment to wildlife conservation projects and working as a field guide.

He has no official home of his own, relying on the generosity of friends and family when he needs a roof over his head and somewhere to write.

Colin also believes we should be here for a good time as it's unlikely to be for a long time; and nobody should have to work for more than six months in any one year. He's made it a personal goal to prove this is possible. So far so good.

www.ingramcontent.com/pod-product-compliance
Lightning Source LLC
Chambersburg PA
CBHW051217160726

47994CB00002B/638